NEW & NATURAL

Vegetables

Elizabeth Brand

BELL & HYMAN

First published 1985 by
Bell & Hyman Limited
Denmark House
37-39 Queen Elizabeth Street
London SE1 2QB

Cover design by Norman Reynolds
Cover photograph by Rob Matheson
Illustrations by Paul Saunders
ISBN 0 7135 2571 1

British Library Cataloguing in Publication Data

Brand, Elizabeth
    Vegetables
    1. Cookery (Vegetables)
    I. Title
    641.6'5   TX801

Typeset by Typecast Ltd., Maidstone.
Printed and bound in Great Britain at The Bath Press, Avon

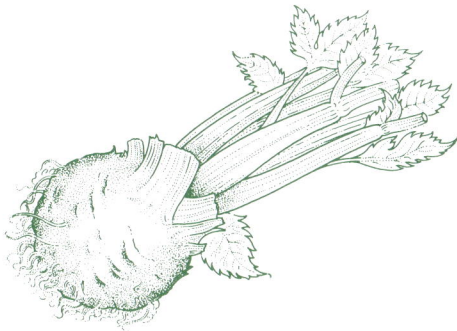

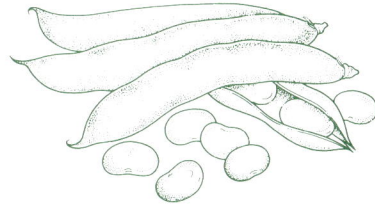

CONTENTS

INTRODUCTION

Vegetables have formed an integral part of our diet for centuries, but never before have we been offered such choice and quality. Sophisticated modern technology has made for more effective cultivation, packaging and transportation techniques, in order that the choicest vegetables are available in as fresh a form as possible.

Fresh vegetables bring with them an unmistakable aura of health and vitality, combined with a wealth of colours — from the rich green leaves of cabbages to the lustrous deep purple of aubergines, and offer an endless range of contrasting textures. Care must be taken during their preparation and cooking to ensure that these characteristics, as well as the vegetable's nutritional value, are preserved. The selection of vegetables is therefore also very important, and guidelines of points to look for when buying are given in the vegetable guide. Paradoxically, price is not a true indication of quality since vegetables tend to be at their best, and least expensive in season, when they are most bountiful.

Renowned for their health giving properties, and despite having a high water content, vegetables are rich in vitamins and minerals, both of which are only needed in small, but nevertheless indispensable, amounts. It is the water soluble vitamins which are particularly vulnerable to unfavourable conditions since boiling is the most common cooking method — either the heat of cooking or the leaching effect of water depletes them. In addition, oxidation (seen in the browning of bruised or cut surfaces) destroys vitamin C. Thus, to minimise loss, vegetables should be bought and prepared just before they are needed, cooked for the minimal time — so that they retain their colour, nutrients and crispness — and served at once.

There is therefore much to be said for the increased use of imaginative salads in the diet. Most vegetables, provided they are cut or shredded finely, can be eaten raw and endless combinations with various dressings can be created. Bland vegetables improve by being served with a piquant dressing — such as *white cabbage and peach salad* tossed in a fresh ginger vinaigrette. The classic green salad — lettuce, cress and endive, with dandelion leaves or lamb's lettuce tossed in for a change, dressed with a French vinaigrette just prior to serving, is quick to prepare and makes a nutritious accompaniment to a main course. However, cooked salads do add another dimension. The vegetables are usually tossed in a dressing while still hot, such as *sweet and sour cauliflower and cabbage salad*, so that the dressing has time to impregnate the vegetables.

Soups, on the other hand, undergo prolonged cooking to draw out as much of the vegetable's flavour as possible. A good stock is the essence of a successful soup, add any vegetables which are to hand — onions, carrots, tomatoes and celery are particularly good, and use water in which vegetables have been cooked so as not to waste the vitamins drawn out during cooking. Swedes, turnips, parsnips and kohlrabi should be avoided because of their overpowering pungent flavour, and starchy vegetables tend to cloud the stock.

The addition of onion and tomato skins and mushroom stalks results in a dark stock — suitable for *carrot, orange and coriander soup.* No commercial soup can hope to emulate the unique flavour of home made ones which offer such diversity, served hot or cold, puréed or chunky, thick or thin, as a main course or starter.

Vegetable dishes make excellent starters, their brightness and freshness stimulating the appetite for the following main course. It is necessary to carefully balance hors d'oeuvre and main course in order to avoid a meal which is too heavy or not filling enough.

Today, more people than ever before are turning towards vegetarianism, mainly as a result of religious, moral or health connotations. In the light of present dietary recommendations to reduce our intake of fat, salt and sugar and increase consumption of fibre, vegetables clearly deserve more of the limelight. They contain negligible amounts, if any, of fat and are high in dietary fibre. Meat is valued as a source of protein (peas and beans being the only vegetables contributing significant amounts of this nutrient), but as a nation we consume more than is necessary, and could therefore afford to reverse the roles which meat and vegetables play in the diet by increasing the consumption of vegetables and reducing or excluding (such as in *Kenya bean lasagne)* that of meat. The chapters on fish, meat and poultry bear this out by using an equal, or higher ratio of vegetables than is usually found. This has the added advantage of economy.

By using more unusual, exotic varieties of vegetables now appearing in shops, as well as traditional ones, the opportunity to make maximum use of the versatility of vegetables is now far greater. The following recipes illustrate how their inclusion adds appeal to both everyday and special occasion cooking.

Acknowledgements

The author and publishers would like to thank the following for the transparencies used in this book.

St. Lucia Products (facing page 24)
The Sea Fish Industry Authority (facing pages 25 and 49)
The Fresh Fruit and Vegetable Information Bureau (facing page 48)

VEGETABLE GUIDE

Globe Artichokes

Available most of the year round, globe artichokes are similar in appearance to large, green-purple thistles. Choose those which have tightly packed heads and show no signs of discolouration or dryness. Artichokes are very popular served as a starter with accompanying dip, or filled with a savoury stuffing. Canned artichoke hearts and bottoms, 'fonds', are becoming increasingly readily available and are particularly good in salads.

Jerusalem Artichokes

Contrary to popular belief, Jerusalem artichokes are not related to globe artichokes. New, larger, easier to peel or scrub varieties are now appearing in shops. Look for firm tubers with a golden skin and as few knobbles as possible. Since peeled artichokes brown in the atmosphere drop into acidulated water after preparing.

Asparagus

White asparagus is considered to be the finest, and imports ensure that it is obtainable most of the year round. Alternatively, French asparagus, with purple flecked tips, and green asparagus, are also available. Look for even sized, unwrinkled, clean stalks with closed tips. Fat stems should be peeled before cooking so that stalks are all the same width.

Aubergines

Also known as 'eggplants', purple, white and green varieties exist although purple aubergines are most prevalent in this country. Even these vary in colour, from light to deep purple, and shape, from round to oval. Ensure that the fruit is unwrinkled, free from blemishes and shiny. Very popular in Mediterranean cuisine, aubergines must be cooked before being eaten and tend to discolour quickly.

Avocados

Although officially a fruit, avocados are used in many vegetable dishes. They are pear shaped with either a smooth green skin, or more oval, with a rough purple skin. Avocados should be slightly soft when squeezed. If not, leave in a warm place for 1-2 days to ripen. Sprinkle cut surfaces with lemon juice to prevent browning.

Bamboo Shoots

These are the inner conical shoots of tropical young bamboo plants. Ivory in colour, with little flavour of their own, they have a crisp texture. Whole or sliced bamboo shoots are sold canned, ready to use.

Beans

Beansprouts

The sprouts of germinating soya or mung beans, beansprouts are white in colour with yellow/green sprouts. 1″-2″ (2.5cm-5cm) in length, they may be eaten raw or cooked. Both fresh and canned varieties are available all year round. Fresh sprouts should look crisp and firm with no trace of water in the packet. Since beansprouts have a very short shelf life they are best consumed on the day of purchase. Beansprouts are easy to grow at home taking 6-8 days to reach maturity.

Bobbi Beans

More rounded in shape than French beans, the slightly fatter pod is a similar length and prepared by breaking off the stem and tip.

Broad Beans

In season from April to September, although canned and frozen varieties are available at all times. Fresh beans are sold unshelled, the shell accounting for roughly half the weight of the pod. Choose those with a crisp, firm, full pod. As with all green vegetables, broad beans are best eaten on the day of purchase. Very young, tender beans need not be shelled. Simply top and tail and remove any fibrous strings before simmering for 15-20 minutes.

French Beans

Nowadays mainly imported from Kenya, and therefore available all year round, French beans ('Haricot vert') are shortish, thin, straight beans which only require topping and tailing before cooking. Look for bright, crisp, velvety pods. Store in the bottom of the refrigerator and eat within 2-3 days of purchase.

Runner Beans

Fresh runner beans are in season from July to September. Longer, and as wide as broad beans, old runner beans will be stringy and tough. To prepare, top, tail and remove fibrous edges before slicing.

Beetroot

Underrated because so often their flavour is masked by sousing in vinegar, beetroots can be served cooked or, finely grated, raw. Available all the year round, their leaves are treated in the same way as spinach. When cooking, scrub beetroot well and leave some of the stem and root end intact, being careful not to pierce the skin, otherwise the beet will 'bleed' and lose some of its distinctive red/purple colour. Uncooked beetroot keeps for several weeks, but for only 2-3 days once cooked.

Broccoli

Purple or white (similar in taste to cauliflower) flowering broccoli are in season during late winter, early spring. Buy firm, fresh looking broccoli which shows no signs of yellowing. Do not keep longer than a couple of days in the refrigerator. Calabrese has fewer leaves, a thicker stalk and denser head of flowers. Imported and home grown, a constant supply of calabrese is ensured.

Brussels Sprouts

Called thus because they were thought to have originated in Belgium near Brussels. Although sprouts are available from September through to March, it is recognised that their flavour improves after a hard frost. Choose dark green, compact buds and eat soon after purchase. Brussels tops are the leaves of the plant and can be used in the same way as spinach.

Cabbage

Chinese Cabbage

Alternatively sold as 'Chinese Leaves', 'Celery Cabbage' or 'Nappa Cabbage', imports ensure its availability all year round. Gaining in popularity, Chinese cabbage keeps for up to 10 days in the refrigerator and has a delicate flavour which is equally good raw or cooked. Look for heavy heads with fleshy white stalks and pale green, crimpled leaves.

Red Cabbage

Readily available during the winter months. Eaten either raw or cooked. When cooked it requires a long, slow method and the addition of a little acid to retain its vibrant purple colour and prevent it turning blue. Red cabbage keeps well, wrap in clingfilm and store in refrigerator once cut.

Savoy Cabbage

Also a winter cabbage. Several varieties, with differing extents of crinkled leaves and compactness of head. Colours ranging from green to purple.

Spring Cabbage

A hardy, leafy variety available, as the name suggests, in spring. The smooth leaves are loosely wrapped around a small conical heart. Choose dark green cabbages which show no sign of yellowing or wilting. Spring greens, also available at this time of year, are simply leaves and have no heart.

White Cabbage

A compact head, similar to the red variety, used in winter salads or boiled. As with red cabbage, the hard central core is cut out before cooking.

Calabrese

See broccoli.

Carrots

A staple English vegetable available throughout the year. Tender early carrots only need scrubbing. Look for smooth carrots, which are free from cracks and store in a cool, dry, dark place for several weeks if necessary.

Cauliflowers

Fresh cauliflowers are available all year, although their price fluctuates — some supermarkets are now stocking just the florets, ready to be cooked. Look for closely packed white heads, free from brown patches, and check that the leaves are green and not yellow. Eat within 2-3 days of purchase.

Celeriac

As its name implies this root vegetable has a similar flavour to celery, to which it is related. Choose smooth roots, to avoid waste when peeling, and ensure that they are relatively heavy for their size. A winter vegetable, in season from October to April, celeriac keeps well for several weeks in a cool, dry place. Drop into water to which a little lemon juice has been added after preparing, to prevent browning.

Celery

Blanched, white celery, or unblanched green varieties are available. Found nearly all year round, choose those with crisp heads and pale green or yellow leaves. Beware of limp, old celery which tends to be stringy and indigestible. To store, separate the stalks and refrigerate for 2-3 days. Canned celery hearts are available from most supermarkets and delicatessens.

Chayote

This gourd is also known as 'Chako', 'Chow Chow', 'Vegetable Pear' or 'Christophene'. Grown in many tropical countries, mainly South America, it resembles a hard green, ribbed pear, which embodies an edible soft, flat seed. Its subtle flavour is a mixture of cucumber, pumpkin and courgette, enabling it to be used for both sweet and savoury dishes. Uncooked chayotes are indigestible.

Sweet Chestnuts

Only available from October to January, although canned and dried forms ensure a constant supply.

When buying, choose large, plump, deep brown chestnuts with a glossy shell. Store for up to two weeks in the larder.

Water Chestnuts

The roots of an oriental water plant, used extensively in Chinese cooking. Available canned in this country, water chestnuts have a bland flavour but distinctive, crunchy texture.

Chicory

A bitter, spear-shaped clump of white leaves with yellow tips, chicory is available all year round, although scarcer during the summer. May be kept for 4-5 days, wrapped, in the refrigerator, thus excluding light which turns the chicory bitter and the leaves green. When buying look for fresh, plump heads. Chicory tends to discolour slightly, so prepare just prior to serving if it is to be eaten raw. Using a small knife remove bitter centre core.

Chillies

These small, hot peppers have been likened to 'wizened fingers' in their shape. Green, yellow, orange and red chillies are available, and as a general guide, the smaller and redder they are, the hotter the taste. Look for firm, shiny pods. Whole dried or powdered chillies may be used for convenience and chilli sauces are popular. Careful preparation when removing the tiny white seeds is

necessary since the chillies are so strong that they 'burn' skin.

Courgettes

Also known as 'Zucchini', these are immature marrows, the difference being that both skin and seeds are edible. Long and thin, they are available all year round, although are best in season, from June to September. Courgettes can be stored for 3-4 days in the larder, but avoid wilted, bruised ones which tend to be bitter.

Cress and Watercress

Both are available all year round but most abundant during the summer. Mustard is often sold sown with cress, and should be left in its punnet until just before serving. Cress and watercress are particularly perishable and should be eaten soon after purchase. When choosing watercress look for crisp, fresh looking leaves and discard any yellowing ones. Trim and wash watercress and keep in a plastic bag in the refrigerator.

Cucumbers

Many different varieties are grown, although shops tend to stock the smooth skinned, long variety grown in greenhouses, which are available all year round. Purchased whole or halved, cucumbers will keep in the bottom of the refrigerator for about a week.

Curly Kale

Much favoured in Scotland, this hardy winter vegetable is available from December to April, and survives the fiercest of frosts. In fact its flavour improves after the first frost. Flat or curly leaved varieties are available.

Dudi

Imported from Kenya and Cyprus, these marrow-like vegetables are either long and thin, some grow to 24″ (60cm), or round, about 4″ (10cm) across. They have pale green skin, which must be peeled before eating, white flesh, edible seeds and a mild flavour. Add dudis to stews, or else steam, boil, fry or bake.

Eddoes

Also known as 'Malangas', this tropical root is mainly imported from the West Indies. Small brown-grey bulbs with side tubers, eddoes have a slightly sticky, starchy, white flesh which has a nutty taste. Use in the same way as potatoes.

Endive

Two varieties of endive are to be found — curly endive, which is available from September to November, and Batavian ('Escarole') endive, which is in season during the winter months until April. Both resemble a curly lettuce in appearance, although Batavian endive has broader less curly leaves, and pale green/yellow hearts due to being tied whilst growing to bleach the centres. Endive has a slightly bitter taste. Look for those which show no signs of wilting and store in a polythene bag for 2-3 days in the refrigerator.

Fennel

Cultivated in Italy, Florence fennel is a bulb, composed of thick, white ribbed leaves, which overlap. The stalks are tinged green and any fern which protrudes from the bulb may be used as an attractive garnish. Fennel has a mild, aniseed flavour and may be stored for 2-3 days in the larder or refrigerator. Imported fennel is available all year round.

Garlic

White or pink skinned garlic is available all year round. Look for bulbs with a white papery skin and plump, unwizened cloves. Puréed garlic, sold in tubes, can now be bought.

Horseradish

This long, thin white root is very pungent when fresh, therefore use sparingly and peel carefully since it tends to 'burn' the skin and eyes.

Kohlrabi

Kohlrabi is a cabbage, ('Kohl' being German for cabbage) with a swollen stem from which shoots protrude. Two main types are available. Purple, which has been grown under glass, and green, grown outside. In season from July to April, their flavour lies between that of turnip and swede. Look for small, smooth-skinned kohlrabi with curly fresh leaves, and eat as soon as possible since they tend to become woody with age. Kohlrabi may be eaten raw or cooked.

Kolocassi

This rhizome is a staple of Africa and Asia. Also known as 'Taro' or 'Dasheen', kolocassi is a large, heavy, starchy vegetable, roughly cylindrical in shape, tapering off at one end. Eaten in the same way as potatoes, kolocassi has a slippery texture, pink-brown bark and a subtle flavour.

Leeks

Available most of the year round, choose medium sized stems with plump white stalks and fresh green leaves. Leeks will keep for up to 3 days in a larder and require thorough washing to remove grit which tends to become lodged between the rings.

Lettuces

Cabbage

The most common in this country and available all year. A round shaped head with soft, loose leaves.

Webbs lettuce is a variety of this group but has a compact head and crisp, ribbed leaves.

Cos

Characterised by long, crisp leaves and a closely packed head. Cos lettuces have a good flavour.

Iceberg

Increasing in popularity. There is very little waste with this variety. The crisp, pale green leaves are clean and densely packed, and will keep in the refrigerator for 1-2 weeks, wrapped in clingfilm. This American lettuce is available all year round although scarcer during the summer.

Lamb's

Also known as 'Corn Salad' or 'Mâche'. So called because its flavour is best when lambing begins, although lamb's lettuce is available all year round. The small, bitter leaves have a delicate flavour and because of their expense are usually incorporated with other green leafy vegetables.

Most varieties of lettuce do not keep well. To store, wash, pat dry and keep in a polythene bag in the refrigerator for 1-2 days. When buying lettuce, look for bright, crisp, green leaves.

Marrow

For years the pride of the gardening enthusiast, marrows are in season from July to October. Their bland flavour benefits from serving with a well flavoured accompaniment. Marrows vary in size and colour, avoid very large ones, since they tend to have little flavour. Unlike courgettes, marrows must be peeled and their seeds removed before eating.

Mooli

See radishes.

Mushrooms

Three main types of the common mushroom exist according to their degree of cultivation.

Button

These are small, closed caps with a delicate flavour and pale colour. Used whole or sliced they are valued for sauces because they do not darken them.

Cup

The gills of these mushrooms are partly open.

Flat or Open

Mature mushrooms with the whole of the dark gills showing. These have the most pronounced flavour.

Due to controlled cultivation, mushrooms are available all year round. Choose those with fresh looking gills — very dark, wet gills and brown caps indicate old, rubbery mushrooms.

Oyster Mushrooms

These imported mushrooms have a slightly tough, meaty texture. Oyster mushrooms are fan-shaped, with no stalks, and fully exposed fawn-grey gills. Look for dry mushrooms which show no signs of curling at the edges. This variety must be cooked before serving.

Okra

Also known as 'Ladies Fingers', 'Gumbo' and 'Bindi', okra is an essential ingredient of Creole cookery. African in origin, these short, slightly hairy, five or six sided green pods which taper to an end, are grown in tropical climates and are most readily available during the summer and autumn. Careful preparation is necessary to avoid puncturing the pod since the mucilaginous juices will then seep out and the pod lose its shape. Store for 2-3 days in the bottom of the refrigerator.

Onions

Pickling, Button or Pearl

Available from July to October, these white, crunchy onions have a mild flavour and are used in pickles. Peeling is made easier by covering them with boiling water for 1 minute, draining and then skinning.

Red, White and Yellow Skinned

Red onions are used in salads and have a mild flavour and deep red skins. Yellow skinned onions are the most popular in this country. Except for red onions, store for several months in a cool, dry place. Buy those with a smooth, papery, bright skin and avoid any which have sprouted.

Shallots

Much prized in France for their flavour, particularly in sauces. In season during the summer months. Peel as for pickling onions.

Spanish

Large, golden skinned onions with a mild flavour, ideal for stuffing. Available all year.

Spring

Look for those with bright green stalks and firm, white bulbs. These are immature onions, mainly used in salads, where both bulb and stalk are eaten. Available all year round.

Palm Hearts

Imported from Brazil, bottled or canned in brine, palm hearts are the smooth, rubbery shoots of the palm tree once the hard outer bark has been removed. Serve as you would asparagus.

Parsnips

In season from September to February, their slightly sweet, nutty flavour improves with a hard frost. Look for medium sized parsnips, with ivory coloured flesh, smooth and firm, with no side shoots or brown patches. The cores of older parsnips are often woody and should be removed before cooking. Store in a cool, dark place for no longer than 2-3 days.

Peas

When buying fresh peas choose small, young, shiny pods which are sweeter because less of their sugar will have had time to turn to starch. The shell accounts for roughly half the pod's weight. Store peas in a vegetable rack or refrigerator for 1-2 days at the most. Fresh peas are available during the summer, otherwise, frozen peas are of good quality.

Mange-tout/Sugar Pea

This variety has tender, flat pods with small seeds. Mange-tout means 'eat all' — to prepare, pull the stalk down the thicker edge thus removing any tough fibres.

Petits Pois

Available from June to September, these are small, young, sweet peas which require less cooking than the later, larger, more floury peas.

Sweet Peppers

Alternatively sold as 'Capsicums' or 'Pimentos', these vary in colour as they ripen from green to yellow, then orange, and finally red, the sweetest. Purple and white varieties are also available. The bitter white pith and seeds must be removed before serving. Peppers are available all year round, buy those with firm, shiny, undamaged skins.

Plantain

Used extensively in West Indian and African cookery, plantain are similar to bananas in appear-ance; green, dry and starchy when unripe, before maturing to yellow and finally black as they increasingly sweeten. Plantain are larger and more fibrous than bananas and must be cooked before being eaten. Use for the same purposes as potatoes — boiled, baked in their skins, or fried.

Potatoes

Many different varieties exist which, according to whether they are floury or waxy, are suited to various methods of cooking. Stay clear of potatoes which show signs of sprouting, are green, or blemished. They will keep well in a cool, dark, dry place. Once peeled cover with water to prevent browning.

New Potatoes

In season from May to August, although imported varieties are available before this. Their tender, almost transparent, skins only require scrubbing to remove excess dirt, and since they are generally small, the potatoes are served whole. Unlike main crop potatoes, new potatoes should be used as soon after purchase as possible. Look for those with slightly moist skins which rub off easily.

Sweet Potatoes

Very popular in America, sweet potatoes can be incorporated in both sweet and savoury dishes. A long, undulating tuber which tapers off to one end, sweet potatoes have a reddish skin and orange, slightly sticky, flesh. Imported from tropical countries, sweet potatoes are available all year round. They only keep for 1-2 weeks before becoming wizened and dried.

Pumpkins

Purchased as a slice, or if of a small variety, whole. Pumpkins are in season from July to November and differ in shape and colour (from green to yellow-orange). Used for both sweet and savoury dishes, uncut pumpkins keep for up to 2 weeks in a larder. Sliced pumpkin should be wrapped in clingfilm and stored in the refrigerator for 1-2 days.

Radishes

Summer radishes, small, red, yellow or white, round or long varieties, with a peppery taste, are sold in bunches. Look for those with fresh green leaves and unbroken skin. Winter radishes, white (such as mooli, also called 'rettich'), brown, purple or black, are larger than the summer varieties and resemble a long, rounded turnip. These tend to be sold individually.

Radicchio

An Italian lettuce, radicchio has small burgundy, slightly bitter leaves, with deep white ribs. It is also known as red chicory. Use sparingly in winter salads. This is quite an expensive vegetable, available from September to April. Look for crisp, bright leaves, and keep for 3-4 days, wrapped in clingfilm, in the refrigerator.

Salsify and Scorzonera

Belonging to the same family, salsify has a white skin and is sometimes called 'Vegetable Oyster' because its smooth texture and flavour are similar to that of oysters, whereas scorzonera has black skin. Resembling a long, thin carrot, with stubble at one end, both have white flesh, which exudes a sticky, milky substance, and once peeled they must be dropped in acidulated water to prevent browning. Available from October to March, buy firm roots, free from excess earth, and store in a larder for 3-4 days.

Sorrel

A green, leafy plant, similar to spinach, but more pronouncedly bitter, sorrel is only available from specialist shops, but can be easily grown at home. In season during the summer months, substitute for spinach in recipes, removing the stem before using.

Spinach

Winter and summer varieties ensure that spinach is available for most of the year. Wash thoroughly to remove grit and discard any leaves which show signs of yellowing. Use as soon as possible.

Swedes

Swedes, like all roots, keep for several weeks in a cool, dark place. Available from September to May, smaller ones have a better flavour.

Sweetcorn

Fresh corn-on-the-cob (maize) is in season from July to November, although canned and frozen kernels, and canned whole baby corns and creamed sweetcorn are available all year round. To remove kernels from cob, peel back leaves, remove silken threads and take a firm hold of the stalk. Slice off kernels, keeping the knife close to the core. One ear yields about 4oz (125g) of kernels. Fresh sweetcorn should not be stored since as soon as it is picked the sugar begins to turn to starch and the cob hardens. Choose pale yellow kernels — plump, bright yellow kernels are more mature and consequently less sweet. When buying make sure that the core is completely covered with kernels and that the green husk looks fresh. The ripe kernels should exude a milky liquid when squeezed.

Swiss Chard

Also called 'Seakale Beet', chard is similar to spinach, but has large, dark green leaves, broad white ribs and a less pronounced flavour. The stalks are usually served separately in the same way as celery.

Tomatoes

Imports guarantee a constant supply of tomatoes. Choose firm, medium sized ones with glossy red skins and rich green stalks. To skin, cover with boiling water for 30 seconds before peeling. Store tomatoes in the refrigerator for up to a week. Green tomatoes may be ripened in a drawer. Low acid yellow tomatoes are sometimes available.

Cherry Tomatoes

Small, round tomatoes, usually served whole in salads, these are also called 'Button Tomatoes'.

Mediterranean Tomatoes

Or 'Beef Tomatoes', these are very large tomatoes with thick flesh and are deeply grooved from the stalk.

Plum Tomatoes

Grown in Italy these are imported canned. A deep red, they have an elongated shape, very few seeds, and are good value.

Turnips

Summer turnips, available from April to July are white, with a hint of green and purple. Winter tur-

nips are in season from August to March. Turnips
should be used soon after purchase, or kept for 1-2
days in a cool, dark place.

Watercress

See cress.

Yams

A tropical tuber with floury white flesh, yams have
a grey-brown bark and may be sold whole or cut.
Use in the same way as potatoes.

SOUPS

Tangy Beetroot and Yoghurt Soup

Serves 8

The brilliant colour of this soup is matched with the pleasing sharpness of yoghurt and lemon juice. Serve chilled. For a change, vegetable crudités, such as small pieces of carrot, cauliflower, green pepper and celery may be handed round with the soup.

1lb (450g) beetroot
1 pint (600ml) cold water
5.29oz (150g) carton natural low fat yoghurt
2 tbsps lemon juice
1 level tsp salt

1. Scrub the beetroot well, being careful not to puncture the skin so that they retain as much of their colour as possible. Place in a pan with water to cover, and simmer, covered, for 1½ hours.

2. Plunge beetroot into cold water. When cool top and tail and remove skin.

3. Place in blender with half the water, yoghurt, lemon juice and salt. Liquidise until smooth. Pour into a large jug, stir in remaining water, cover, and refrigerate until very cold.

Carrot, Orange and Coriander Soup

Serves 6

Carrots, subtly flavoured with orange and coriander, make a beautifully colourful soup. Serve with warm wholemeal cheese rolls.

1lb (450g) carrots
6oz (175g) onion
2 medium oranges
1 tbsp vegetable oil
1½ pints (900ml) vegetable stock
2 level tbsps finely chopped coriander
1 level tsp salt
pepper

1. Peel and thinly slice carrots. Peel and finely chop onion. Finely grate oranges and squeeze juice.

2. Heat oil. Add carrot and onion. Cover, and sauté for 10 minutes, without browning. Shake pan occasionally.

3. Add orange zest and juice, stock, coriander and seasoning. Bring to the boil, cover, and simmer for 45 minutes.

4. Cool slightly. Pour into blender and purée until smooth. Return to pan and reheat.

Cauliflower and Ginger Soup

Serves 8

Cauliflower, flavoured with just a hint of ginger, takes on a unique delicate flavour. You may wish to add more ginger according to your personal taste. Serve hot with wholemeal soda bread.

2½lbs (1.1kg) cauliflower
6oz (175g) onion
½oz (15g) fresh root ginger
1oz (25g) margarine
1 tsp vegetable oil
1½ pints (900ml) vegetable stock
1½ level tsps salt
pepper

1. Slice off cauliflower base, and discard discoloured outer leaves. Thinly slice remaining leaves and break cauliflower into florets. Wash and drain well.

2. Peel and finely chop onion and ginger.

3. Heat margarine and oil. Add cauliflower and onion, cover, and sauté, without browning, for 10 minutes. Shake pan occasionally.

4. Add ginger, stock, salt and pepper, bring to the boil cover, and simmer for 30 minutes. Cool slightly.

5. Place soup in blender and liquidise until smooth. Return to pan, reheat and serve.

Celery and Apricot Soup

Serves 6

An unusual blend of flavours which takes the edge off celery's otherwise rather distinctive taste. Serve with wholegrain cheese biscuits.

1lb (450g) celery
4oz (125g) onion
4oz (125g) dried apricots
½oz (15g) margarine
1 tsp vegetable oil
1½ pints (900ml) vegetable stock
½ level tsp salt
pepper

1. Trim celery, wash and thinly slice. Peel and finely chop onion. Finely chop apricots.

2. Heat margarine and oil. Add celery and onion, cover, and sauté, without browning, for 10 minutes. Shake pan occasionally.

3. Add apricots, stock and seasonings, bring to the boil, cover, and simmer for 45 minutes. Cool slightly.

4. Place in a blender and liquidise until smooth. Return to pan and reheat.

Pumpkin Soup (page 27)

Cheshire, Leek and Nutmeg Soup

Serves 6

A warming winter vegetable soup, enriched with a sprinkling of creamy Cheshire cheese. Serve with hunks of freshly baked wholemeal bread.

1lb (450g) leeks
1½lbs (700g) potatoes
3oz (75g) coloured Cheshire
1oz (25g) margarine
1 tsp vegetable oil
1 pint (600ml) vegetable stock
½ level tsp salt
⅛ level tsp nutmeg
¼ pint (150ml) milk

1. Trim leeks, using as much of the green stalk as possible. Slice into ¼″ (6mm) rings, wash thoroughly in cold water, drain. Peel potatoes and slice into ¼″ (6mm) slices. Grate cheese.

2. Heat margarine and oil. Add leeks and potatoes, cover, and sauté, without browning, for 10 minutes. Shake pan occasionally.

3. Add stock, salt and nutmeg. Bring to the boil, cover, and simmer for 35 minutes. Cool slightly. Place in blender and liquidise until smooth.

4. Return to pan. Add milk and bring back to the boil. Spoon into individual soup bowls and sprinkle with a little cheese.

Chunky Bobbi Bean, Tomato and Mushroom Soup

Serves 4

Good enough to serve as a main course, this soup is delicious served hot or cold, accompanied with fresh, crusty wholemeal rolls.

4oz (125g) onion
1lb (450g) tomatoes
6oz (175g) button mushrooms
6oz (175g) Bobbi, or French beans
1oz (25g) margarine
1 pint (600ml) vegetable stock
2 level tbsps finely chopped parsley
1 level tsp thyme
1 level tsp soft brown sugar
½ level tsp salt
pepper

1. Peel and finely chop onion. Skin tomatoes and dice into ¼″ (6mm) cubes. Wash and dry mushrooms, leave whole, unless they are large. Wash, drain, top and tail beans. Slice diagonally into ½″ (12.5mm) lengths.

2. Melt margarine. Add onion and fry for 2-3 minutes. Stir in vegetables, stock, parsley, thyme, sugar, salt and pepper.

3. Bring to the boil, cover, and simmer for 30 minutes.

Quick Vegetable Scallop Fry (page 40)

Cucumber, Pea and Mint Soup

Serves 4

The peas give this soup a nutty texture which is delicious when served hot. Alternatively serve chilled with wholemeal French bread. You will probably find that the vegetables give the soup so much flavour that no seasoning is necessary.

4oz (125g) onion
1lb (450g) fresh peas in their pods,
  6oz (175g) shelled weight
8oz (225g) cucumber
1oz (25g) margarine
1 pint (600ml) vegetable stock
1 level tbsp finely chopped mint
sprigs of mint to garnish

1. Peel and finely chop onion. Shell, wash and drain peas. Wipe cucumber and dice into ½″ (12.5mm) cubes.
2. Melt margarine. Add onion, peas and cucumber, cover, and sauté for 10 minutes without browning. Shake pan occasionally.
3. Pour in stock and stir in chopped mint. Cover, and simmer for 45 minutes.
4. Cool slightly, liquidise and return to pan. Reheat and serve garnished with sprigs of mint.

Red Gazpacho Soup

Serves 8

Quick to make and requiring no cooking, here Gazpacho soup is served with toasted wholemeal breadcrumbs which should be handed round separately, or sprinkled over the soup just prior to serving.

1lb (450g) tomatoes
4oz (125g) red pepper
2oz (50g) red onion
1 clove garlic
2 tbsps vegetable oil
11½ fl oz (330ml) can tomato and vegetable juice
¾ pint (450ml) cold water
1 tbsp lemon juice
½ level tsp salt
¼ level tsp paprika
¼ level tsp ground cumin
2oz (50g) wholemeal breadcrumbs

1. Skin and roughly chop tomatoes. Wipe pepper, remove stalk and seeds, roughly chop. Peel and roughly chop onion. Peel and crush garlic. Place all ingredients in blender with oil. Process until very finely chopped.
2. Pour into a large jug, add tomato and vegetable juice, water, lemon juice, salt, paprika and cumin. Stir well, cover, and chill.
3. Brown breadcrumbs under grill and serve with soup.

Cream of Jerusalem Soup with Walnuts

Serves 4

A delicate, pale soup, best served with very thin slices of wholemeal toast.

1lb (450g) Jerusalem artichokes
1 tsp lemon juice
4oz (125g) onion
½oz (15g) margarine
1 tsp vegetable oil
¾ pint (450ml) water
½ level tsp salt
pepper
¼ pint (150ml) milk
1oz (25g) finely chopped walnuts

1. Peel artichokes, halve, and drop into a basin of cold water with lemon juice.

2. Peel and finely chop onion. Heat margarine and oil. Drain artichokes and add to pan with onion. Sauté, covered, for 10 minutes, without browning. Shake pan occasionally.

3. Add water and seasonings. Bring to the boil, cover, and simmer for 30 minutes. Allow to cool slightly.

4. Place in blender and liquidise until smooth. Return to pan. Add milk, and bring to the boil. Ladle into individual bowls and sprinkle with chopped nuts.

Pumpkin Soup

Serves 8

A truly frugal, yet flavoursome, soup. For a crunchy topping, the pumpkin seeds can be toasted in the oven at 180°C (350°F), gas 4 for 20 minutes and scattered over the soup just before serving.

3lbs (1.4kg) pumpkin
12oz (350g) onions
1tsp vegetable oil
1oz (25g) margarine
1 pint (600ml) vegetable stock
1 level tsp salt
½ level tsp ground coriander
¼ level tsp cinnamon
1 level tbsp finely chopped parsley

1. Peel pumpkin, remove seeds and pith. Dice into 1″ (2.5cm) cubes. Peel and finely chop onion.

2. Heat oil and margarine. Add pumpkin and onion. Sauté, covered, for 10 minutes, without browning. Shake pan occasionally.

3. Add stock, salt, coriander and cinnamon. Bring to the boil, cover, and simmer for 30 minutes.

4. Allow to cool slightly. Liquidise until smooth. Return to pan and heat through before serving. Garnish with finely chopped parsley.

Sumptuous Summer Soup

Serves 8

Despite having an excellent flavour when cooked in a similar way to cabbage, all too often lettuce is relegated to monotonous and unimaginative use in salads. This soup is best made during summer when lettuce is cheap and plentiful. Use three cobs of fresh sweetcorn instead of canned if preferred, and serve hot with crispbreads.

8oz (225g) onions
1oz (25g) margarine
1½lbs (700g) Webbs lettuce
12oz (340g) can sweetcorn and peppers
2 pints (1.2 litres) vegetable stock
1 level tsp salt
pepper
1 level tbsp sunflower seeds

1. Peel and finely chop onion. Melt margarine and fry onion for 3-4 minutes.

2. Wash and drain lettuce. Shred finely and add to onion. Cover, and sauté for 5 minutes, shaking pan occasionally.

3. Drain sweetcorn and peppers and add, with stock and seasonings. Bring to the boil, cover, and simmer for 45 minutes.

4. Roast sunflower seeds under a hot grill until lightly toasted, about 2-3 minutes.

5. Spoon soup into individual bowls and sprinkle with sunflower seeds.

Winter Vegetable Soup

Serves 10

Chunky root vegetables provide the basis of this soup. For a satisfying meal, serve with hunks of wholemeal bread and Cheddar.

12oz (350g) parsnips
12oz (350g) swede
12oz (350g) turnips
12oz (350g) carrots
6oz (175g) onion
4oz (125g) barley
2oz (50g) margarine
2½ pints (1.5 litres) water
2½ level tsps salt
pepper

1. Peel parsnips, swede, turnips, carrots and onion. Dice into ¼" (6mm) cubes.

2. Melt margarine in a large saucepan. Add vegetables and sauté, covered, for 10 minutes, without browning. Shake pan occasionally.

3. Stir in barley, water and seasonings. Bring to the boil, cover, and simmer for 1 hour.

STARTERS

Stuffed Baked Artichokes

Serves 4

Reminiscent of an oriental flower — the outer leaves encase a vibrant red centre — these artichokes make an enchanting hors d'oeuvre. If preferred they may be served plain; after simmering in stock, drain and serve with vinaigrette.

4 medium globe artichokes
2 tsps lemon juice
½ pint (300ml) vegetable stock
8oz (225g) onions
1lb (450g) tomatoes
8oz (225g) red pepper
3 tbsps vegetable oil
1 level tsp oregano
½ level tsp salt
pepper
4oz (125g) lean cooked ham

1. Wash and drain artichokes. Slice 1″ (2.5cm) off the head. Cut off stem and tough outer leaves. Neaten remaining leaf tops with scissors. Sprinkle with lemon juice to prevent browning.

2. Stand artichokes upright in a tightly fitting pan and pour in stock to come half way up sides. Bring to the boil, cover, and simmer for 20-25 minutes until tender, and the leaves can be pulled out easily. Drain and allow to cool slightly.

3. Pull back outer leaves to reveal hairy choke. Pull out the fibres to expose the greyish base. Leave until cold.

4. Peel and finely chop onions. Peel and roughly chop tomatoes. Wipe pepper. Remove stalk and seeds and finely chop. Heat 1 tablespoon oil. Add onions and fry for 3-4 minutes. Add tomatoes, pepper, oregano, salt and pepper. Bring to the boil, and simmer, covered, for about 25 minutes, or until pulpy. Cool.

5. Grease an ovenproof dish. Preheat oven 180°C (350°F), gas 4.

6. Finely chop ham. Stir into tomato mixture. Pack filling into artichoke centres. Reshape and place in prepared dish. Sprinkle with remaining oil. Cover, and bake for 20 minutes. Remove cover and cook for a further 15-20 minutes.

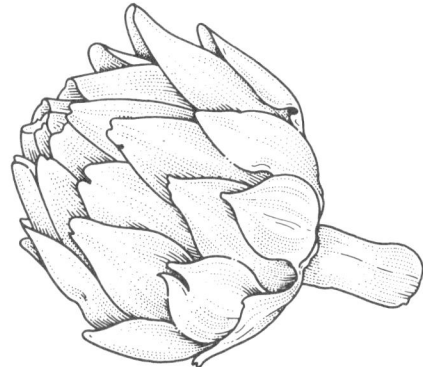

Asparagus with Watercress Hollandaise

Serves 4

There is no substitute for the flavour of real butter here. Serve this rich green sauce in a bowl surrounded with a plate of the asparagus spears.

1lb (450g) asparagus spears
1 bunch watercress
3oz (75g) butter
2 (size 3) egg yolks
1 tbsp white wine vinegar
¼ level tsp salt
pepper

1. Remove 1″ (2.5cm) from the bottom end of each asparagus stem. Starting from the bottom, thinly peel so that the stalks are of an even size.

2. Wash, dry and very finely chop watercress. Melt butter and allow to cool to blood heat.

3. Tie asparagus spears in a bundle with some string to prevent the heads from knocking against each other and cook, covered, in boiling water for 7-8 minutes. Remove from water, untie and drain well on kitchen paper.

4. Place egg yolks and vinegar in blender. Liquidise until thoroughly mixed. Add half the warm butter, drop by drop, through the lid. Pour in remainder in a trickle with the blender still running.

5. Transfer sauce to a double saucepan. Add chopped watercress and seasonings and stir over barely simmering water until the sauce thickens, about 4-5 minutes. Serve warm with asparagus spears.

Egg and Aubergine Pumpernickel Rafts

Serves 4

Fried aubergines, topped with tarragon flavoured scrambled eggs and served on nutty dark pumpernickel bread make a filling hors d'oeuvre and are delicious as a snack.

12oz (350g) aubergine
½oz (15g) seasoned flour
6 tbsps vegetable oil
4 slices Pumpernickel bread, measuring 4½″ × 3½″
  (12cm × 9cm)
4 (size 3) eggs
4 tbsps milk
½ level tsp tarragon
½ level tsp salt
pepper
1oz (25g) margarine
tarragon to garnish

1. Wipe aubergine. Discard stalk and slice into ¼″ (6mm) thick rounds. Coat in seasoned flour.

2. Heat 3 tablespoons of the oil in a frying pan. Add half the aubergines and fry for 2-3 minutes on both sides, until crisp and golden. Remove and keep warm. Add remaining oil and fry uncooked aubergines, drain and keep warm.

3. Lightly toast pumpernickel bread.

4. Whisk together eggs, milk, tarragon and seasonings. Melt margarine, add egg mixture and cook over a low heat, stirring continuously, until the eggs are almost set.

5. Arrange aubergine slices on toasted pumpernickel. Spoon scrambled egg on top and sprinkle with a little tarragon. Serve at once.

Chequered Avocado

Serves 4

A colourful hors d'oeuvre, composed of cubes of green, yellow, red and brown, and served on individual plates, this can be made up to 3 hours in advance.

2oz (50g) button mushrooms
2oz (50g) Cheddar cheese
2oz (50g) red pepper
2 medium avocados
2 tbsps vegetable oil
1 tbsp tarragon vinegar
1 tsp lemon juice
¼ level tsp salt
pepper
1 clove garlic

1. Wash, dry and dice mushrooms into ¼" (6mm) cubes. Dice cheese into similar sized cubes. Wipe pepper, remove stalk and seeds. Dice into ¼" (6mm) cubes. Halve avocados, carefully remove flesh from skin, and dice into ¼" (6mm) cubes.

2. Whisk together oil, vinegar, lemon juice, salt and pepper. Peel and crush in garlic.

3. Stir mushrooms, cheese, pepper and avocado into dressing. Mix thoroughly. Pile back into shells and serve.

Avocado, Ham and Egg Salad Hors d'Oeuvre

Serves 4

The textures of avocado, ham and egg mingle pleasantly to produce a stimulating starter.

2 medium avocados
4oz (125g) cooked ham
3 (size 3) hard boiled eggs
3 tbsps vegetable oil
1 tbsp tarragon vinegar
1 level tsp Dijon mustard
¼ level tsp salt
black pepper

1. Halve avocados, remove stones and carefully ease flesh away from skin. Dice into ¼" (6mm) cubes. Slice ham into thin strips, 1" (2.5cm) long. Shell eggs and chop roughly. Combine with avocado and ham.

2. Whisk together oil, vinegar, mustard, salt and pepper. Toss avocado mixture in dressing.

3. Just before serving pile mixture back into avocado shells.

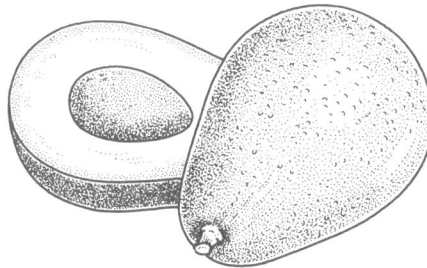

Celery and Sesame Spread

Makes 1lb (450g)

This crunchy, creamy spread can be served as pâté, potted in small ramekins, or as 'eats', on wholewheat crackers or bridge rolls.

6oz (175g) celery
1oz (25g) sesame seeds
8oz (225g) cream cheese
¼ level tsp salt
⅛ level tsp paprika

1. Trim, wash, and chop celery very finely in blender/ processor.

2. Toast sesame seeds under a high grill for 3-4 minutes until light brown. Cool.

3. Beat cheese until smooth. Add celery, sesame seeds, salt and paprika. Mix well. Pot, cover, and chill before using.

Corn with Barbecue Sauce

Serves 4

Fresh corn on the cob is served here with a piquant golden barbecue sauce, as an alternative to the traditional melted butter.

2oz (50g) onion
1 clove garlic
8oz (225g) tomatoes
4oz (125g) green pepper
1oz (25g) green chillies

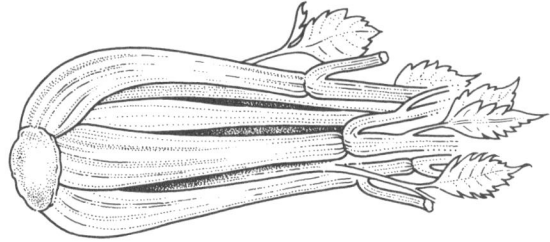

½oz (15g) fresh root ginger
1oz (25g) margarine
1 level tbsp tomato purée
2 tsps malt vinegar
1 tsp Worcestershire sauce
¼ pint (150ml) vegetable stock
1 level tsp muscovado sugar
¼ level tsp salt
4 medium corn on the cob
2 tbsps dry sherry

1. Peel and finely chop onion. Peel and crush garlic. Skin and roughly chop tomato. Wipe pepper and chillies, remove stalks and seeds, and chop finely. Peel and grate ginger.

2. Melt margarine. Add onion and garlic. Fry for 2-3 minutes. Stir in tomato, pepper, chilli, ginger, tomato purée, vinegar, Worcestershire sauce, stock, sugar and salt.

3. Bring to the boil, cover, and simmer for 30 minutes, removing lid for last 10 minutes of cooking. Cool slightly before puréeing through a sieve.

4. Slice stalks from cobs. Remove leaves and silky threads. Place in a pan of boiling salted water and simmer, covered, for 20 minutes, or until tender. Drain.

5. Meanwhile, return sauce to pan, bring back to the boil, add sherry and simmer for 2-3 minutes. Pour over cobs and serve.

Lemony Courgette Croustades

Makes 12

These intriguing individual bread cases make an unusual appetiser for any occasion. Serve with slices of seasoned tomato.

12oz (350g) courgettes
12 slices thinly cut wholemeal bread
2oz (50g) margarine
5.29oz (150g) carton natural low fat yoghurt
finely grated peel of ½ medium lemon
¼ level tsp salt
⅛ level tsp nutmeg

1. Grease 12 Yorkshire pudding tins. Preheat oven 200°C (400°F), gas 6.

2. Wipe courgettes and dice into ¼″ (6mm) cubes. Blanch in boiling salted water for 2 minutes. Rinse under cold water, drain well.

3. Trim crusts from bread. Flatten slices with a rolling pin until very thin. Use to line pudding tins, firmly flattening out as many of the creases in the bread as possible, with fingertips.

4. Melt margarine and use to liberally brush bread cases. Bake for 10-15 minutes until crisp. Carefully remove from tins and cool on a wire rack.

5. Whisk together yoghurt, lemon peel, salt and nutmeg. Stir in courgettes and spoon mixture into bread cases.

Cucumber and Tarragon Dip

Makes 8 fl oz (225ml)

Serve a variety of thinly sliced, raw vegetables with this fresh tasting dip. Celery, cauliflower, radishes, cooked globe artichoke leaves, carrot and green pepper could be included.

6oz (175g) cucumber
1 level tsp salt
5.29oz (150g) carton natural set yoghurt
1 level tsp tarragon
cayenne pepper

1. Wipe cucumber, dice into ¼″ (6mm) cubes. Place in a bowl, sprinkle with salt and leave to stand for 1 hour so that water runs from cucumber and leaves it crisp. Wash well under cold water to remove salt. Drain thoroughly.

2. Place in blender/processor, and liquidise until almost smooth. Expel any excess moisture by placing cucumber in a sieve, and squeezing liquid out.

3. Mix cucumber with yoghurt, tarragon and pepper. Serve in a bowl, surrounded with the crudités, attractively arranged.

Leek and Gruyere Tartlets

Makes 12

Hand these individual tarts around with drinks to stimulate your guests' appetites for what's to follow. Serve either hot or cold.

8oz (225g) leeks, approximately 4oz (125g)
  trimmed weight
1oz (25g) margarine
4oz (125g) wholemeal flour
½ level tsp salt
1oz (25g) vegetable fat
1oz (25g) margarine
4 tsps cold water
3oz (75g) Gruyere cheese
2 (size 3) eggs
¼ level tsp salt
nutmeg

1. Preheat oven, 200°C (400°F), gas 6.

2. Slice leeks very thinly. Wash and drain well. Melt margarine. Add leeks and sauté, uncovered, for 8 minutes, without browning, until tender. Cool slightly.

3. Place flour and salt in a bowl. Rub in fat and bind to a stiff dough with water. Turn out onto a lightly floured surface and knead until smooth. Cover and chill for 15 minutes.

4. Grate cheese, add leeks, eggs, salt and a pinch of nutmeg. Whisk together.

5. Roll out pastry on a lightly floured surface. Using a 3″ (7.5cm) cutter press out 12 circles. Use to line 12 bun tins.

6. Spoon a little mixture into each pastry case. Bake for 15 minutes until the cheese has melted and is golden.

Port Marinaded Marrow

Serves 6

Port has the effect of softening marrow whilst at the same time imparting a subtle flavour to it, thus making it difficult to distinguish whether the vegetable is in fact marrow, melon or cucumber. A little goes a long way, so spoon a small amount into individual glasses and serve with wholegrain crisp rolls, or a similar wheat crispbread.

2lbs (900g) marrow
10 juniper berries
¼ pint (150ml) port
1 level tsp soft brown sugar
6 sprigs mint

1. Slice stalk and end from marrow, peel, halve lengthways and scoop out seeds. Dice into ½″ (12.5mm) cubes. Crush juniper berries.

2. Place marrow in a bowl with junipers, port and sugar. Leave to marinate for 6-8 hours, or in a cool place overnight. Stir occasionally.

3. Remove juniper berries. Divide marrow and marinade between six individual, small wine glasses. Garnish with sprigs of mint.

Mexican Vegetable Tortillas

Makes 12

Tortillas add a new dimension to barbecues or informal drinks parties. The fillings may be varied, try using grated raw carrot instead of sweetcorn, and substituting beansprouts for lettuce.

12 fl oz (350ml) water
1oz (25g) margarine
4oz (125g) corn meal
6oz (175g) wholemeal flour
1 level tsp salt
4oz (125g) onion
4oz (125g) green pepper

1oz (25g) green chillies
8oz (225g) tomatoes
15.25oz (432g) can red kidney beans
3oz (75g) lettuce
4oz (125g) Cheddar cheese
2 tsps vegetable oil
4oz (125g) sweetcorn kernels
½ level tsp ground coriander
½ level tsp salt
¼ level tsp ground cumin
¼ level tsp paprika
2 tbsps water

1. Place water and margarine in a pan. Bring to the boil, stir in corn meal and cook over a low heat, covered, for 5 minutes. Cool slightly. Knead in wholemeal flour and salt to a smooth dough.

2. Turn out onto a lightly floured surface, roll out very thinly, until almost transparent and, using a 6½″ (17cm) plate as a guide, cut out 12 circles. Cover with clingfilm.

3. Peel and finely chop onion. Wipe pepper and chillies, remove stalks and seeds, chop finely. Skin and roughly chop tomatoes. Drain kidney beans. Wash, dry and finely shred lettuce. Grate cheese.

4. Heat oil. Add onion and fry for 2-3 minutes. Stir in pepper, chillies, tomatoes, beans, sweetcorn, seasonings and water. Bring to the boil and simmer, uncovered, for 20 minutes, stirring occasionally, until liquid has evaporated.

5. Meanwhile, warm a frying pan over a moderate heat. Fry one tortilla at a time, for 2-3 minutes on each side, until flecked with brown spots. Wrap in a dry teatowel.

6. Holding tortilla shell, cupped in palm of hand, spoon in a rounded tablespoonful of bean mixture, top with a little lettuce and a sprinkling of cheese. Repeat with remaining tortilla shells and serve at once.

Mediterranean Mushrooms

Serves 4

The fresh, delicate flavour of juicy button mushrooms is enhanced by a light oil and tomato dressing. Serve in small ramekin dishes, sprinkled with plenty of finely chopped parsley.

6oz (175g) tomatoes
1oz (25g) celery
1 clove garlic
8oz (225g) button mushrooms
2 tbsps olive oil
1 tbsp lemon juice
sprig of parsley
bayleaf
¼ pint (150ml) water
¼ level tsp salt
pepper
1 level tbsp finely chopped parsley

1. Skin tomatoes, de-seed and finely chop. Wipe celery and cut in half. Peel and crush garlic. Wash and dry mushrooms.

2. Place tomatoes, celery, garlic, oil, lemon juice, parsley sprig, bayleaf, water and seasoning in a pan. Bring to the boil and simmer, uncovered, for 5 minutes.

3. Add mushrooms and simmer, uncovered, for a further 5 minutes. Remove celery, parsley and bayleaf. Using a slotted spoon divide mushrooms between 4 small ramekin dishes.

4. Boil liquid rapidly, uncovered, for 5 minutes until reduced by about half. Spoon over mushrooms and sprinkle with parsley.

Lemon and Garlic Stuffed Mushrooms

Serves 4

Serve these moist, tender mushrooms on a round of toasted wholemeal bread. If wished the mushrooms may be sprinkled with 1 level tablespoon wholemeal breadcrumbs before baking.

4 large flat mushrooms, approximately 4" (10cm)
  in diameter
2oz (50g) margarine
1 clove garlic
2 level tbsps finely chopped parsley
finely grated peel of ½ lemon
¼ level tsp salt
pepper

1. Lightly grease a baking sheet. Preheat oven 190°C (375°F), gas 5.

2. Wash and dry mushrooms. Trim stalks and chop finely.

3. Beat margarine until soft. Peel and crush garlic, stir into margarine with mushroom stalks, parsley, lemon peel, salt and pepper.

4. Divide mixture between mushrooms and spread evenly over flat side of mushrooms.

5. Place on baking sheet and cook, uncovered, for 20 minutes. Serve at once.

Chunky Mushroom and Egg Pâté

Serves 8

Serve with triangles of freshly made wholemeal toast.

8oz (225g) button mushrooms
4 (size 3) hard boiled eggs
1 level tsp paprika
½ level tsp salt
4 level tbsps whipped cream

1. Wash mushrooms. Place in a pan of boiling water and simmer, covered, for 5 minutes. Drain well and allow to cool.

2. Halve and thinly slice mushrooms. Peel eggs and grate. Place mushrooms, egg, paprika, salt and cream in a bowl. Mix well.

3. Pot, and chill before serving.

Crumbed Okra with Red Pepper and Tomato Sauce

Serves 4

Choose medium, even sized okra, which will cook at the same speed. The heat of the oil results in the breadcrumbs forming a crisp casing for these intriguingly shaped bright green pods.

4oz (125g) onion
12oz (350g) tomatoes
4oz (125g) red pepper
1 tbsp vegetable oil
bayleaf
¼ pint (150ml) vegetable stock
½ level tsp salt
pepper
4oz (125g) okra
2 (size 3) eggs
2oz (50g) stale wholemeal breadcrumbs
1 level tbsp toasted sesame seeds
1 level tsp oregano
1 level tbsp seasoned wholemeal flour
vegetable oil for deep fat frying

1. Peel and finely chop onion. Peel and roughly chop tomato. Wipe pepper. Remove stalk and seeds, chop finely.

2. Heat oil, add onion, and fry for 2-3 minutes. Stir in tomato, pepper, bayleaf, stock and seasonings. Bring to the boil and cook rapidly, uncovered, for 15 minutes, until pulpy.

3. Meanwhile, wash and dry okra. Carefully cut off stem without revealing seeds.

4. Lightly whisk eggs. Mix together breadcrumbs, sesame seeds and oregano.

5. Coat okra in flour, followed by egg, and then the breadcrumb mixture. Repeat egg and breadcrumb stage.

6. Heat oil for frying. Fry six 'fingers' at a time, for 2 minutes, until crisp and golden. Drain on crumpled kitchen paper. Serve at once with sauce.

Neapolitan Vegetable Mousse

Serves 6

Tofu imparts a smooth, creamy texture to the trio of green, orange and white vegetables without detracting attention from their flavour. Serve with a selection of crunchy wholegrain cheese biscuits.

8oz (225g) cauliflower
8oz (225g) carrots
8oz (225g) shelled peas
10½oz (297g) carton silken Tofu
salt
pepper

1. Grease 6 small ramekin dishes. Have ready a water bath with boiling water. Preheat oven 160°C (325°F), gas 3.

2. Trim leaves from cauliflower. Divide into florets. Wash and drain. Cook in boiling water for 15 minutes. Drain.

3. Peel and thinly slice carrots. Place in a pan with a little water, bring to the boil and simmer for 15 minutes. Drain.

4. Cook peas in boiling water for 10 minutes. Drain.

5. Drain Tofu. Place ⅓ in blender with cauliflower and seasoning to taste. Process until smooth. Spoon into a bowl. Repeat with carrots and then peas, spooning each into separate bowls.

6. Place alternate spoonfuls of mixture into greased dishes, end with all three colours showing on the top. Cover with foil, stand in water bath and cook for 30 minutes. Remove foil and serve hot.

Peppered Noodles with Pea Sauce

Serves 8

Tender young peas colour this cream sauce a delicate pale green. Topped with crispy bacon and served on a bed of noodles, this makes an attractive starter.

1lb (450g) fresh peas in their pods, 6oz (175g)
*   shelled weight*
4oz (125g) onion
4oz (125g) green streaky bacon
4fl oz (125ml) vegetable stock
½ level tsp soft brown sugar
¼ level tsp salt
8oz (225g) wholewheat noodles or tagliatelle
½oz (15g) margarine
freshly ground black pepper
5fl oz (142ml) carton soured cream

1. Shell, wash and drain peas. Peel and finely chop onion. Remove rind from bacon and snip into small strips.

2. Bring stock to the boil. Add peas, onion, sugar and salt, cover, and simmer for 20 minutes. Allow to cool slightly. Liquidise contents of pan until smooth.

3. Cook noodles in a pan of boiling salted water for 5-6 minutes. Drain well. Toss in margarine and black pepper.

4. Fry bacon in its own fat until crisp and golden, about 5 minutes. Drain.

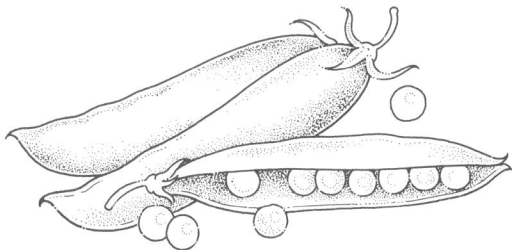

5. Return sauce to pan, bring back to the boil, remove from heat and stir in cream.

6. Place noodles in a warmed shallow serving dish. Pour sauce over top and sprinkle bacon down the centre. Serve immediately.

Herby Beef Tomatoes

Serves 8

A simple, light starter for a summer dinner party when Mediterranean tomatoes are at their best. Use fresh herbs if you can and serve with slices of wholemeal garlic bread.

4 Mediterranean tomatoes, approximate weight
*   2½lbs (1.1kg)*
1oz (25g) onion
1 clove garlic
1oz (25g) wholemeal breadcrumbs
4 level tbsps finely chopped parsley
1 level tbsp finely chopped basil
1 level tbsp finely chopped thyme
½ level tsp salt
pepper
2 tsps vegetable oil

1. Preheat oven 200°C (400°F), gas 6.
2. Wipe tomatoes, halve horizontally and scoop out fleshy pulp, leaving a ¼″ (6mm) thick shell. Turn upside down on a piece of kitchen paper, and leave to drain while preparing filling. Finely chop pulp.

3. Peel and finely chop onion. Peel and crush garlic clove. Place in a bowl with tomato pulp, onion, breadcrumbs, parsley, basil, thyme and seasonings. Mix thoroughly.

4. Spoon mixture into tomato shells. Drizzle ¼ teaspoon oil over each and bake, uncovered, for 10-15 minutes.

Sardine Salad Pitta Bread

Serves 4

Crunchy wholemeal pitta bread filled with radish, cucumber, sardine and egg, provides a lunchtime snack in itself. Alternatively, serve halves as a starter at informal gatherings. These are best eaten straight away while the pitta is crisp.

4oz (125g) radishes
4oz (125g) cucumber
4.37oz (134g) can sardines in soya oil
2 (size 3) hard boiled eggs
1 tbsp white wine vinegar
¼ level tsp salt
⅛ level tsp paprika
4 wholemeal pitta breads

1. Trim, wash and grate radishes. Wipe and grate cucumber. Drain sardines and reserve oil. Halve, remove backbone, and flake fish into small pieces. Shell and grate hard boiled eggs. Add egg and sardine to vegetables, mix well.

2. Place 2 tablespoons sardine oil, vinegar and seasonings in a pan. Slowly bring to the boil, pour over salad and toss ingredients until evenly coated.

3. Preheat grill on high. Grill pitta bread until lightly browned and slightly puffed up, about 2 minutes on each side.

4. Slit pitta horizontally. Divide vegetable mixture evenly between breads and spread into each pocket. Serve at once.

Jellied Tomato, Spinach and Egg Ring

Serves 6

A quick, easy to make, yet attractive dinner party hors d'oeuvre. Serve with wholemeal Melba toast.

0.85oz (24g) packet aspic
18fl oz (500ml) tomato juice
½ level tsp salt
pepper
2 (size 3) hard boiled eggs
8oz (225g) spinach
bunch of watercress

1. Wet a 2 pint (1.2 litre) ring mould.

2. Dissolve aspic in ¼ pint (150ml) tomato juice. Stir into remaining juice, season.

3. Pour a little tomato juice into the bottom of the prepared mould. Thinly slice hard boiled eggs and arrange, overlapping, in the tomato juice. Refrigerate until set.

4. Wash spinach in several changes of cold water. Drain, place in a large saucepan, cover and cook for 6-7 minutes until leaves are limp. Drain well and purée.

5. Stir spinach into remaining tomato juice and pour over egg slices. Refrigerate until set.

6. Dip mould in a basin of hot water for 30 seconds. Invert onto a serving dish. Wash, drain and trim watercress. Arrange in centre of mould.

Quick Vegetable Scallop Fry

Serves 2

Stir-fried vegetables provide a colourful contrast for these tasty scallops. A special occasion hors d'oeuvre, serve with crusty, warm garlic bread.

4 scallops
1oz (25g) seasoned flour
2oz (50g) spring onions
2oz (50g) celery
2oz (50g) courgette
2oz (50g) carrots
1oz (25g) margarine
salt
pepper

1. Wash and dry scallops. Remove coral, slice in half. Cut the white flesh into thin slices. Toss coral and white flesh in seasoned flour.

2. Trim spring onions and celery. Slice thinly. Wipe courgette and slice thinly. Peel carrots and cut into strips.

3. Melt margarine and gently fry scallops for 3 minutes. Stir in spring onion and celery and fry for a further 2 minutes, adding a little more margarine if necessary. Add courgette and carrot. Cook until just tender. Season to taste and serve at once.

SALADS

Tangy Asparagus Salad

Serves 2

Tender asparagus spears, topped with crunchy herb breadcrumbs make an exclusive side salad for rich cold meats such as pork and lamb.

8oz (225g) asparagus spears
1oz (25g) margarine
1 tsp vegetable oil
2oz (50g) wholemeal breadcrumbs
1 level tsp thyme
1 tbsp vegetable oil
finely grated zest of ½ lemon and 1 tbsp juice
⅛ level tsp salt
pepper

1. Remove 1″ (2.5cm) from the bottom of each asparagus stem. Starting from the bottom, peel so that stalks are of an even thickness.

2. Tie spears in a bundle to prevent heads from knocking against each other. Cook, covered, in boiling water for 7-8 minutes. Remove spears and drain well on a piece of kitchen paper. Allow to cool.

3. Heat margarine and oil. Stir in breadcrumbs and thyme, fry over a high heat for about 5 minutes, or until golden brown. Drain and cool.

4. Arrange asparagus on a serving plate. Scatter breadcrumbs over the top.

5. Whisk together remaining ingredients and hand dressing round separately.

Speckled Aubergine Salad

Serves 4

Fresh horseradish root gives a kick to this salad, so use sparingly. Serve with chopped hard boiled eggs and crusty French bread.

1lb (450g) aubergines
1 tsp lemon juice
4 rounded tbsps mayonnaise
1 level tbsp tomato purée
1 level tbsp poppy seeds
2 level tsps soft brown sugar
1 tsp white wine vinegar
¼ level tsp very finely chopped horseradish
¼ level tsp salt

1. Wipe aubergines and remove stalk. Dice into ½″ (12.5mm) cubes. Cook, covered, for 5 minutes, in a pan of boiling water with lemon juice. Drain well and allow to cool.

2. Whisk together mayonnaise, tomato purée, poppy seeds, sugar, vinegar, horseradish and salt.

3. Toss aubergine in dressing. Serve.

Avocado, Mushroom and Bacon Salad

Serves 6

Serve this avocado and mushroom salad in garlic vinaigrette, topped with crispy bacon, as a starter or accompaniment to cold meats.

2oz (50g) smoked streaky bacon
4oz (125g) button mushrooms
2 medium avocados
2 small cloves garlic
2 tbsps vegetable oil
1 tbsp tarragon vinegar
1 level tsp made mustard
½ level tsp caster sugar
¼ level tsp salt

1. Remove rind from bacon. Snip into thin strips and fry in its own fat until crisp. Drain and cool.
2. Wash, dry and thinly slice mushrooms.
3. Peel avocados. Remove stones and slice thinly. Arrange, overlapping, around the edge of serving plate. Pile mushrooms in centre.
4. Peel and crush garlic cloves. Whisk with oil, vinegar, mustard, sugar and salt. Pour over salad and scatter bacon over top.

Beetroot and Orange Salad

Serves 6

Buying cooked beetroot saves a great deal of preparation time. If you are using uncooked beets, simmer covered, in a pan of water, for 1½ hours. Serve with hard boiled eggs and a selection of cooked meats.

1lb (450g) cooked beetroot
1 orange
4 rounded tbsps mayonnaise
1 tsp white wine vinegar
¼ level tsp salt
pepper

1. Peel beetroot and dice into ¼″ (6mm) cubes.
2. Finely grate orange peel and squeeze the juice.
3. Whisk together orange peel, 2 tablespoons orange juice, mayonnaise, vinegar and seasoning.
4. Toss beetroot in dressing.

Broad Bean Salad

Serves 4

A main course in itself. Serve with wafer thin crispbreads to fully appreciate the complementary flavours of this salad.

12oz (350g) shelled broad beans
3 tbsps vegetable oil
1 tbsp white wine vinegar
3 level tbsps finely chopped parsley
¼ level tsp salt
¼ level tsp dry mustard
pepper
4oz (125g) lean cooked ham
2 (size 3) hard boiled eggs

1. Simmer broad beans, covered, for 20-25 minutes. Drain.
2. Whisk together oil, vinegar, parsley, salt, mustard and pepper. Toss beans in dressing while they are still hot. Cover and allow to cool.
3. Slice ham into 1″ (2.5cm) long strips. Shell hard boiled eggs and cut, lengthways, into 8. Stir into beans with ham.

Calabrese and Tomato Salad with White Cheese Dressing

Serves 6

Particularly suitable for slimmers, this salad is comprised of low fat cheeses with 'meaty' chunks of crisp vegetables which provide a delicious, filling salad.

1lb (450g) calabrese
12oz (350g) tomatoes
6oz (175g) onion
5oz (150g) low fat soft cheese
2 level tbsps skimmed milk
½ level tsp Dijon mustard
¼ level tsp salt
cayenne pepper
4oz (125g) low fat Cheshire cheese

1. Cut florets from thick calabrese stalks. Divide into small clusters. Shred stalks into 2″ (5cm) long, matchstick strips. Wash and drain. Blanch in boiling water for 4 minutes. Run under cold water and drain thoroughly.

2. Cut tomatoes into thin wedges. Peel and halve onion, slice into thin semicircles. Blanch in boiling water for 1 minute. Drain.

3. Combine all vegetables in a bowl.

4. Whisk together soft cheese, milk, mustard, salt and pepper. Crumble in Cheshire cheese. Pour dressing over vegetables and mix well.

Red Cabbage and Apple Salad

Serves 8

A colourful, crunchy, winter salad, which goes well with cold roast pork.

1lb (450g) red cabbage
8oz (225g) eating apples
4oz (125g) raisins
3 tbsps vegetable oil
1 tbsp white wine vinegar
1 tbsp lemon juice
½ level tsp powdered cloves
¼ level tsp salt

1. Finely shred cabbage. Wash and drain well. Peel, core, and dice apples into ¼″ (6mm) cubes.

2. Place cabbage, apples and raisins in a bowl, mix thoroughly.

3. Whisk together remaining ingredients and toss salad in dressing.

White Cabbage, Peach and Ginger Salad

Serves 6

The subtle ginger flavouring in this salad makes it an excellent accompaniment to cold meats, especially chicken and pork.

1lb (450g) white cabbage
1 tub cress
2 medium peaches
1 tbsp lemon juice
1oz (25g) fresh root ginger
3 tbsps vegetable oil
1 tbsp white wine vinegar
¼ level tsp salt

1. Shred cabbage. Wash and drain cress. Halve, stone and thickly slice peaches. Sprinkle with lemon juice.

2. Peel ginger and press through a garlic crusher. Whisk together oil, vinegar and salt and stir in ginger.

3. Mix cabbage, cress and peaches in a bowl. Toss salad in dressing.

Sweet and Sour Cauliflower and Cabbage Salad

Serves 6

Reminiscent of the oranges, coppers and fading greens of autumn, this winter salad goes well with cold meats and rice.

1½lbs (700g) cauliflower
12oz (350g) Primo cabbage
8oz (225g) can whole water chestnuts
8oz (227g) can pineapple slices in natural juice
1 level tsp cornflour
1 level tsp soft brown sugar
2 tbsps malt vinegar
1 tbsp soy sauce
1 tbsp water
1 level tbsp tomato purée
2 tsps sherry

1. Trim outer leaves and stalk from cauliflower. Divide into small florets, shred leaves, wash and drain. Discard any discoloured cabbage leaves, cut cabbage into ¼″ (6mm) thick slices, wash and drain. Drain chestnuts and slice thinly. Drain pineapple, reserve juice, cut rings into eight.

2. Cook cauliflower and cabbage, covered, in boiling salted water, for 4 minutes. Drain well.

3. Blend cornflour and sugar with remaining ingredients. Place in a pan with water chestnuts, pineapple chunks and juice. Bring to the boil and simmer for 2-3 minutes.

4. Pour sauce over cauliflower and cabbage. Stir well, cover, and allow to cool.

Celeriac and Carrot Salad with Mustard Seed Dressing

Serves 8

This rich winter salad makes an interesting filling for jacket potatoes, sprinkled with freshly chopped parsley.

1¼lbs (600g) celeriac
1 tsp lemon juice
12oz (350g) carrots
2oz (50g) sultanas
2 rounded tbsps mayonnaise
2 rounded tbsps soured cream
2 level tsps Meaux mustard
¼ level tsp salt

1. Peel celeriac thickly. Cut into matchstick sized pieces. Place in a bowl of water with lemon juice to prevent browning.

2. Peel carrots and cut into the same size strips.

3. Drain celeriac and blanch with carrot in boiling water for 4 minutes. Plunge into cold water. Drain well.

4. Stir sultanas into vegetables.

5. Whisk together mayonnaise, cream, mustard and salt. Toss salad in dressing.

Celery and Carrot Salad

Serves 6

Walnut vinaigrette combines well with grated celery and carrot to give a crunchy textured salad. Accompany with any light meat.

12oz (350g) celery
12oz (350g) carrots
2 oz (50g) walnuts
3 tbsps vegetable oil
1 tbsp white wine vinegar
2 level tbsps finely chopped parsley
¼ level tsp salt
pepper

1. Wash and coarsely grate celery. Peel and coarsely grate carrots. Roughly chop nuts.

2. Whisk together remaining ingredients and toss vegetables in dressing.

Chiffon Salad

Serves 6

Grated mooli and radish, combined with crisp alfalfa sprouts and curly endive make an attractive, delicate looking salad. Lightly seasoned with curry powder, this salad goes well with roast chicken.

8oz (225g) mooli
5oz (150g) radishes
6oz (175g) curly endive
4oz (125g) alfalfa salad sprouts
4 tbsps vegetable oil
2 tbsps malt vinegar
1 level tsp Madras curry powder
1 level tsp soft brown sugar
¼ level tsp salt

1. Peel and coarsely grate mooli. Trim, wash and dry radishes, grate.

2. Wash and drain endive. Shred finely. Wash and drain alfalfa sprouts. Mix with mooli, radishes and endive.

3. Whisk together remaining ingredients and toss salad in dressing.

Chinese Salad
Serves 6

The Chinese are renowned for their ability to match unusual, contrasting flavours and textures. This salad emulates their style by combining pea pods, sweetcorn kernels, spring onions and nuts with the more bitter beansprouts and pepper, and tossing the ingredients in a sharp soy dressing. Delicious with strips of egg omelette, roast chicken quarters or barbecued spare ribs.

4oz (125g) mange-tout
4oz (125g) sweetcorn kernels
8oz (225g) Chinese leaves
4oz (125g) beansprouts
4oz (125g) green pepper
2oz (50g) cashew nuts
2oz (50g) spring onions
4 tbsps vegetable oil
1 tbsp malt vinegar
1 tbsp lemon juice
2 tsps soy sauce

1. Remove stalks from mange-tout. Blanch in boiling water for 4 minutes. Run under cold water to prevent further cooking. Drain.

2. Blanch corn for 3-4 minutes until tender. Run under cold water. Drain.

3. Cut Chinese leaves lengthways into 3, then cut across into thin strips. Wash and drain. Place in a large bowl with mange-tout, sweetcorn and beansprouts.

4. Wipe pepper, remove stalk and seeds. Cut into thin strips, about 1½" (4cm) in length. Add to salad with cashews, which have been lightly toasted, and thinly sliced spring onions.

5. Whisk together remaining ingredients and toss salad in dressing.

Indian Cucumber Salad
Serves 4

Serve as an accompaniment to hot or cold lamb dishes. This salad has a distinctive taste so keep in reserve for special occasions!

12oz (350g) cucumber
1 level tsp salt
5.29oz (150g) carton natural low fat yoghurt
1oz (25g) flaked coconut
1oz (25g) sultanas
finely grated zest of 1 lime
⅛ level tsp ground coriander

1. Wipe cucumber. Dice into ½" (12.5mm) cubes. Place in a bowl, sprinkle with salt and leave to stand for 1 hour so that water runs from cucumber and leaves it crisp. Wash well under cold water to remove salt. Drain thoroughly.

2. Mix together remaining ingredients and stir in cucumber.

Florida Salad
Serves 4

As an alternative, mix together the chopped segments of 2 small oranges, 2oz (50g) stoned, chopped dates and 12oz (350g) cottage cheese with the pineapple and arrange in the centre of a cartwheel of iceberg lettuce wedges. Serve this refreshing salad as a main course with brown rice.

1 small, fresh pineapple
6oz (175g) celery
½ bunch spring onions
1 green pepper
1 avocado
8oz (225g) cooked ham
6 tbsps vegetable oil

3 tbsps cider vinegar
finely grated rind of 1 lime and 1 tbsp juice
salt
pepper
1 small lettuce

1. Peel pineapple and cut flesh into cubes. Trim celery and spring onions, wash and thinly slice. Wipe pepper, remove stalk and seeds. Chop. Peel avocado, remove stone and slice thinly. Dice ham into similar sized cubes to pineapple.

2. Whisk together oil, vinegar, lime rind and juice, salt and pepper. Toss pineapple, celery, spring onions, pepper, avocado and ham in dressing. Arrange lettuce leaves on a serving plate and spoon prepared salad into centre.

Flower Salad
Serves 8

A centre of lychees surrounded by leafy red raddichio and white chicory leaves makes a spectacular flower centrepiece salad for any dinner party. The slight bitterness of chicory and raddichio being counteracted by the sweet lychees and raspberry vinegar.

3 heads chicory, approximate weight 10oz (275g)
4oz (125g) raddichio leaves
15oz (425g) can lychees or 18 fresh lychees,
 peeled and stoned
3 tbsps vegetable oil
3 tbsps raspberry vinegar
1 level tsp soft brown sugar
½ level tsp salt
pepper

1. Separate chicory leaves. Wash and drain, arrange around the edge of a large oval plate.

2. Separate raddichio leaves. Wash and drain, arrange, overlapping, inside chicory.

3. Drain lychees and pile into centre.

4. Whisk together oil, vinegar, sugar and seasonings. Pour evenly over salad.

Leek Log Salad with Red Pepper Dressing
Serves 4

Red pepper turns the mayonnaise dressing a beautiful pink colour and imparts a subtle sweetness to the 'oniony' flavoured leeks. Serve as a side salad to accompany steamed or poached fish.

1lb (450g) leeks
4oz (125g) red pepper
¼ pint (150ml) mayonnaise
¼ level tsp salt

1. Trim leeks 1″ (2.5cm) above green stalk. Cut into 1″ (2.5cm) barrels. Wash and drain, blanch in boiling water for 4 minutes. Run under cold water, drain well.

2. Slit barrels in half horizontally. Arrange, cut side down, on a serving dish, reserving one piece of leek for garnish.

3. Wipe pepper, remove stalk and seeds, finely chop. (A food processor is ideal for this). Mix with mayonnaise and salt. Pour over leeks.

4. Thinly shred reserved leek and sprinkle over salad.

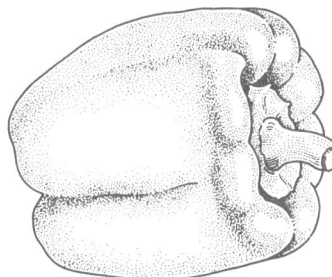

Mediterranean Salad with Tofu Dressing

Serves 6

Tofu has a creamy taste and soft, smooth consistency which makes it an ideal dressing for salads since it only requires blending. Its subtle flavour is enhanced here with oregano, and it is used to coat chunky pieces of cucumber, tomato and black olives. Serve with steamed fish, and wholemeal pitta bread.

10oz (275g) cucumber
8oz (225g) cherry/button tomatoes
6 black olives
10½oz (297g) packet Tofu soyabean curd
1 level tsp oregano
½ level tsp salt
pepper

1. Wipe cucumber. Slice into ¼" (6mm) thick rings. Divide each into 8 wedges.

2. Wash and dry tomatoes.

3. Halve and stone olives. Mix with cucumber and tomatoes.

4. Blend Tofu until smooth. Add oregano and seasonings and toss salad in dressing.

Mushroom, Courgette, Tomato and Butterbean Salad

Serves 8

The crispness of young courgettes contrasts well with the softer texture of tomatoes, mushrooms and butterbeans, whilst adding toasted sesame seeds gives an unexpected nutty texture to the salad. Serve with grated Cheddar.

6oz (175g) dried butterbeans
1lb (450g) courgettes
12oz (350g) tomatoes
6oz (175g) button mushrooms
4 tbsps vegetable oil
2 tbsps white wine vinegar
1 level tsp soft brown sugar
½ level tsp salt
¼ level tsp dry mustard
pepper
1oz (25g) sesame seeds

1. Soak butterbeans overnight in plenty of cold water. Drain. Place in a pan, cover with water, bring to the boil, cover, and simmer for about 1¼ hours. Drain.

2. Wipe courgettes, remove stalk and dice into ¼" (6mm) cubes. Dice tomatoes into the same sized cubes. Wash, dry and thinly slice mushrooms.

3. Combine butterbeans, courgettes, tomatoes and mushrooms in a bowl.

4. Whisk together oil, vinegar and seasonings. Lightly toast sesame seeds under a grill, stir into dressing. Toss vegetables in vinaigrette.

Florida Salad (page 46)

Overleaf: Crunchy Topped Vegetable and Fish Parcels (page 71)

Parsnip and Cranberry Salad

Serves 6

The sharpness of cranberries contrasts with the sweetness of parsnips to given a piquant, rosy salad. If you have the ingredients to hand use leftover parsnips, cranberry sauce and soured cream, and serve with slices of cold Christmas turkey.

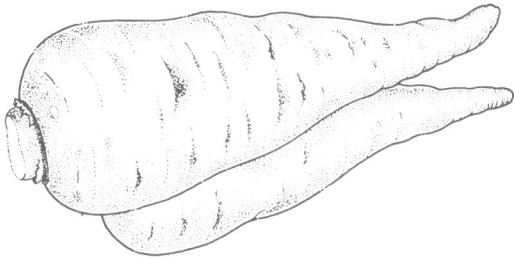

1½lbs (700g) parsnips
4oz (125g) cranberries
1 tbsp port
1 level tsp clear honey
5fl oz (142 ml) carton soured cream
¼ level tsp salt

1. Peel parsnips and dice into ½″ (12.5mm) cubes. Wash and drain cranberries.

2. Place parsnips in a pan of salted water, bring to the boil, cover, and simmer for 10-12 minutes, until just tender. Drain and allow to cool.

3. Place cranberries, port and honey in a small pan, cover, and poach for 10 minutes until soft. Cool.

4. Stir soured cream and salt into cranberries. Toss parsnips in dressing.

New Potato Salad

Serves 6-8

Turn the most mundane potato salad into something special with this tart, cooked egg sauce. Delicious served with a selection of cooked meats or smoked fish.

2lbs (900g) small new potatoes
½ pint (285ml) carton buttermilk
2 (size 3) eggs
1oz (25g) margarine
1 level tbsp cornflour
1 level tbsp white wine vinegar
1 level tsp light soft brown sugar
¼ level tsp salt
cayenne pepper
2 level tbsps finely chopped chives

1. Scrub potatoes. Place in a pan with just enough water to cover. Bring to the boil, cover, and simmer for 12-15 minutes until tender. Drain well.

2. Meanwhile, place buttermilk in a small pan. Beat eggs and add with margarine, cornflour, vinegar, sugar, salt and a pinch of cayenne.

3. Bring slowly to the boil, add chives and simmer for 2-3 minutes.

4. Pour sauce over warm potatoes, cover, and allow to cool.

Snow Salad

Serves 6-8

One of the delights of vegetable cookery is being able to obtain a unique flavour by amalgamating two distinctly different vegetables. Artichoke hearts and kohlrabi marry well to provide an intriguing winter salad. Serve with wafer thin slices of cold roast beef, to give a contrasting colour to the salad without masking its definite taste.

6oz (175g) brown rice
¾ pint (450ml) water
¾ level tsp salt
2 tbsps vegetable oil
1 tbsp tarragon vinegar
pepper
8oz (225g) kohlrabi
14oz (397g) can artichoke hearts
2 (size 3) hard boiled eggs

1. Wash rice and drain well. Place water in a pan with ½ level tsp salt. Bring to the boil, add rice and simmer, covered, for 30 minutes until the water has been absorbed and rice cooked.

2. Meanwhile, whisk together oil, vinegar, and remaining salt and pepper. Stir in rice while still hot. Cover, and leave until cold.

3. Peel and grate kohlrabi. Drain artichoke hearts and quarter. Peel hard boiled eggs and slice, lengthways, into 8.

4. Add kohlrabi, artichoke hearts and egg to rice, mix thoroughly.

Vegetable Bulghur Salad

Serves 6-8

Bulghur has a delicious flavour and texture of its own, which is far superior to that of its nearest equivalent, rice. Comprised of a medley of colours and dressed with a mint vinaigrette, this is a stunning salad to serve with grilled chicken, hard boiled eggs or poached fish.

4oz (125g) bulghur
¾ level tsp salt
8fl oz (225ml) water
4 tbsps vegetable oil
2 tbsps white wine vinegar
1 level tbsp finely chopped mint
pepper
6oz (175g) French beans
4oz (125g) red pepper
2oz (50g) Brazil nuts
7oz (198g) can sweetcorn

1. Rinse bulghur. Place in a pan with ½ level teaspoon salt and water. Bring to the boil, cover, and simmer for 8 minutes, or until the water has absorbed and bulghur is cooked.

2. Whisk together oil, vinegar, mint, remaining salt and pepper. Toss bulghur in dressing while still hot. Cover, and allow to cool.

3. Wash, top and tail beans and slice, diagonally, into ½" (12.5mm) lengths. Blanch in boiling water for 4 minutes. Run under cold water to prevent further cooking, drain well.

4. Wipe pepper. Remove stalk and seeds. Cut into thin strips, about ½" (12.5mm) in length. Slice Brazil nuts into thin slithers and toast until golden. Drain sweetcorn.

5. Stir beans, pepper, nuts and sweetcorn into bulghur.

VEGETABLE DISHES

Almond Aubergines with Chilli Sauce

Serves 4

These aubergine slices, coated in almond batter, are very filling, so two circles each will be plenty. Accompany with steamed cauliflower and lightly cooked cabbage.

4oz (125g) onion
1oz (25g) green chillies
12oz (350g) tomatoes
1 tbsp vegetable oil
¼ pint (150ml) vegetable stock
½ level tsp salt
¼ level tsp paprika
8oz (225g) aubergine
2oz (50g) wholemeal flour
¼ level tsp salt
pepper
1oz (25g) ground almonds
2 tsps vegetable oil

6 tbsps cold water
1 (size 3) egg white
vegetable oil for deep fat frying

1. Peel and finely chop onion. Remove stem and seeds from chillies. Finely chop. Skin and roughly chop tomatoes.

2. Heat oil. Add onion and chilli, fry for 2-3 minutes. Stir in tomato, stock, salt and paprika. Bring to the boil and cook rapidly, uncovered, for 15 minutes, until pulpy.

3. Meanwhile, wipe aubergine. Remove stalk and slice into ¼" (6mm) thick circles.

4. Place flour, salt, pepper and ground almonds in a bowl. Mix well. Add oil and water, and mix to a smooth batter. Stiffly whisk egg white and fold into batter.

5. Heat oil for frying. Thinly coat aubergine slices with batter. Fry three circles at a time, for about 3 minutes, until puffy and golden. Drain on crumpled kitchen paper and serve at once with chilli sauce.

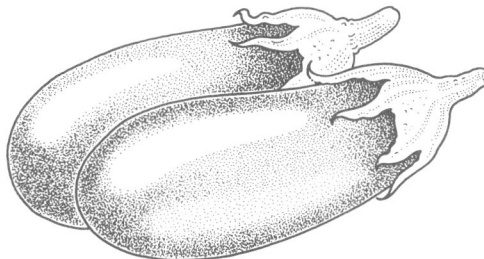

Kenya Bean and Emmental Lasagne

Serves 4

The Kenya beans give this dish a surprising crunchy texture and provide a welcome alternative to the traditional layer of mince. Serve piping hot with a green salad.

4oz (125g) onion
1lb (450g) tomatoes
1 clove garlic
8oz (225g) Kenya beans
10oz (275g) Emmental cheese
1oz (25g) margarine
½ pint (300ml) vegetable stock
1 level tsp tomato paste
½ level tsp basil
1 bayleaf
1 level tsp soft brown sugar
1 level tsp salt
pepper
4oz (125g) precooked spinach lasagne

1. Grease a 2¾ pint (1.6 litre) deep ovenproof dish. Preheat oven 190°C (375°F), gas 5.

2. Peel and finely chop onion. Skin and roughly chop tomatoes. Peel and crush garlic. Wash beans, top and tail, blanch in boiling salted water for 5 minutes. Drain. Grate cheese.

3. Melt margarine. Add onion and fry for 3-4 minutes. Stir in tomato, garlic, stock, tomato paste, basil, bayleaf, sugar, salt and pepper. Simmer, uncovered, for 30-35 minutes, until sauce has reduced to a thick pulp. Remove bayleaf.

4. Spoon a quarter of tomato sauce over base of dish. Make a layer with a third of the lasagne sheets, covered with another quarter of sauce, a third of the beans and a third of cheese. Repeat layers twice.

5. Bake lasagne for 30 minutes until golden and cheese has melted.

Broad Bean Burgers

Makes 12

Full of fibre, these healthy burgers are packed with a mixture of broad beans, sesame seeds and hazelnuts. Serve with home-made tomato or barbecue relish and watercress.

12oz (350g) shelled broad beans
4oz (125g) onion
1 clove garlic
2 tsps vegetable oil
2oz (50g) hazelnuts
1oz (25g) sesame seeds
4oz (125g) wholemeal breadcrumbs
½ level tsp marjoram
½ level tsp salt
pepper
1 (size 3) egg
oil for grilling

1. Grease a grill pan.

2. Cook beans, covered, in a little simmering water, for 15-20 minutes. Drain well. Mince in a blender/processor, until almost smooth. Leave to cool.

3. Peel and mince onion and garlic. Heat oil. Add vegetables and cook for 2-3 minutes until soft. Cool.

4. Toast hazelnuts and sesame seeds until brown. Grind in a blender/processor.

5. Place beans, onion and garlic mixture, ground nuts and seeds, breadcrumbs, marjoram and seasonings in a bowl. Mix well. Lightly beat egg and use to bind mixture together.

6. Divide into 12 and shape into burgers, 3" (7.5cm) in diameter, and ½" (12.5mm) thick. Preheat grill on high. Brush burgers with oil and grill for 3 minutes on each side, until crisp and golden.

Cheesy Beetroot Flan

Serves 6

All too often the delicate flavour of beetroot is spoilt by sousing it in vinegar. Beetroot goes well with cheese, and cooked in a walnut pastry makes a deliciously unusual dish. Serve hot or cold with a green salad.

6oz (175g) wholemeal flour
¼ level tsp dry mustard
¼ level tsp salt
1½oz (40g) vegetable fat
1½oz (40g) margarine
2oz (50g) finely chopped walnuts
approximately 2 tbsps cold water
1lb (450g) cooked beetroot
2 (size 3) eggs
¼ pint (150ml) milk
4oz (125g) Red Leicester cheese
¼ level tsp salt
pepper

1. Preheat oven 220°C (425°F), gas 7.

2. Sift flour, mustard and salt into a bowl. Rub in fat, stir in chopped walnuts and bind to a stiff dough with water. Turn out onto a lightly floured surface and knead until smooth. Roll out and use to line a 9" (23cm) flan dish. Line pastry with foil and bake blind for 15 minutes, removing the foil after 10 minutes.

Remove from oven and reduce temperature to 200°C (400°F), gas 6.

3. Meanwhile, peel beetroot and slice into thin wedges. Whisk together eggs and milk. Grate cheese and add to mixture with seasonings.

4. Arrange beetroot wedges, overlapping, over base of pastry case. Pour egg mixture over beetroot and return to oven for a further 30 minutes, until the egg mixture has set.

Spicy Carrot Loaf

Makes a 2lb (900g) loaf

To fully appreciate the subtle eastern flavours of this carrot loaf, serve slices with a crisp green salad, tomatoes seasoned with black pepper, and a mild soft cheese.

8oz (225g) carrots
8oz (225g) wholemeal flour
2½ level tsps baking powder
½ level tsp salt
½-1 level tsp garam masala
4oz (125g) margarine
2 level tbsps finely chopped coriander
1 (size 3) egg
6 tbsps milk

1. Grease and line a 2lb (900g) loaf tin. Preheat oven 180°C (350°F), gas 4.

2. Peel and finely grate carrots.

3. Sift flour, baking powder, salt and garam masala into a bowl. Rub in margarine.

4. Stir in carrots and coriander. Beat egg and add to dry ingredients with milk. Mix thoroughly with a fork.

5. Spoon into prepared tin, level surface and bake for 1 hour until an inserted skewer comes out clean. Allow to cool in tin for 10 minutes before turning out onto a wire rack.

Chard Leaves with Fruit and Nut Rice

Serves 4

Chard leaves provide an ideal envelope for all kinds of stuffings —, here is a prune and pine kernel filling. Cooked in fresh tomato sauce this makes an excellent summer dish, served with boiled new potatoes and young carrots.

4oz (125g) onion
1 clove garlic
1lb (450g) tomatoes
3oz (75g) celery
1oz (25g) stoned prunes
1oz (25g) margarine
½ pint (300ml) vegetable stock
bayleaf
½ level tsp salt
½ level tsp soft brown sugar
2oz (50g) brown rice
1oz (25g) pine kernels
¼ level tsp nutmeg
¼ level tsp salt
8 large chard leaves

1. Preheat oven 180°C (350°F), gas 4.

2. Peel and finely chop onion, peel and crush garlic. Skin tomatoes and roughly chop. Wash, dry and finely chop celery. Chop prunes.

3. Melt margarine. Add onion and garlic and fry for 3-4 minutes. Stir in tomatoes, stock, bayleaf, salt and sugar. Bring to the boil, cover, and simmer for 30 minutes. Remove lid 10 minutes before end of cooking time. Discard bayleaf.

4. Rinse rice. Cook in boiling salted water for 15 minutes. Drain.

5. Mix celery and prunes with rice, pine kernels, nutmeg and salt.

6. Wash and dry chard leaves. Remove white stalks, cutting 4″ (10cm) of the thick white centre vein from the leaf as well so that it can be easily rolled up.

7. Place a rounded tablespoon of the rice mixture in the centre of each leaf, where the vein starts. Fold vein end, then both sides of the leaf over filling, roll up tightly.

8. Pack parcels into a shallow ovenproof dish and pour tomato sauce over leaves. Cover with foil and bake for 45 minutes.

Coachman's Savoy Bake

Serves 6

One for autumnal days this! Bright green savoy cabbage leaves encase a light pumpkin and cheese mousse centre, delicious served with jacket potatoes.

2½lbs (1.1kg) pumpkin
4oz (125g) Cheshire cheese
1 clove garlic
3 (size 3) eggs
1 level tsp salt
nutmeg
8oz (225g) savoy cabbage leaves

1. Grease a 2¾ pint (1.65 litre) pie dish. Have ready a water bath with boiling water. Preheat oven 190°C (375°F), gas 5.

2. Peel pumpkin, remove seeds and pith. Dice into 1" (2.5cm) cubes. Cook in boiling water to cover for 20 minutes. Drain well.

3. Grate cheese. Peel and crush garlic. Place in blender with pumpkin, cheese, eggs, salt and a pinch of nutmeg. Liquidise until smooth.

4. Wash cabbage leaves. Blanch in boiling water for 8 minutes. Drain well. Use half the leaves to line the pie dish, making sure they overlap to keep in the pumpkin purée, and come just above the top of the dish.

5. Pour half the pumpkin purée into the dish. Cover with some of the leaves, reserving a few for the top. Pour in remaining purée and place reserved cabbage leaves over top.

6. Fold outer leaves over top leaves, cover dish with foil to hold leaves in place. Stand in water bath and cook for 50 minutes.

7. Remove dish from water bath, take off foil, and invert pumpkin bake onto a warmed serving dish.

Nutty Leek and Tomato Shortbread

Serves 6

Slices of leek and tomato in a smooth white sauce provide a contrasting topping for the crisp cashew nut shortbread base. Serve hot with boiled potatoes and carrots, tossed in parsley, or cold, as part of a packed lunch, or picnic feast.

4oz (125g) wholemeal flour
½ level tsp salt
3oz (75g) margarine
2oz (50g) chopped cashew nuts
1 (size 4) egg
1lb (450g) leeks
12oz (350g) tomatoes
2oz (50g) plain flour
¼ pint (150ml) milk
¼ level tsp salt
pepper

1. Grease an 8" (20cm) sandwich tin. Preheat oven 190°C (375°F), gas 5.

2. Place wholemeal flour and salt in a bowl. Rub in 2oz (50g) fat, add nuts, lightly beaten egg and bind to a stiff dough. Press evenly into prepared tin, and bake for 20 minutes.

3. Trim leeks 1" (2.5cm) above green stalk. Slice into ¼" (6mm) thick rings. Wash and drain well. Skin tomatoes and slice thinly.

4. Melt remaining margarine, add leeks and cook for 10 minutes, covered, until soft, but not brown. Add flour and cook for 2-3 minutes. Blend in milk, bring to the boil, stir in tomato and seasonings, simmer for 1-2 minutes.

5. Remove shortbread from oven. Spread leek mixture over surface, and return to oven for a further 15 minutes.

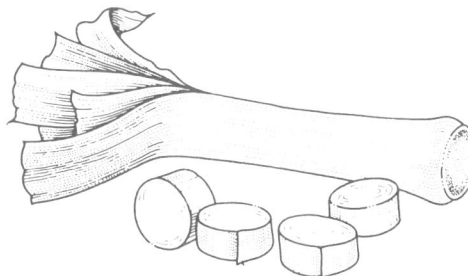

Mushroom Choux Puffs

Serves 4

Serve either hot or cold accompanied by a tomato and chive salad.

5oz (150g) flat mushrooms
2oz (50g) onion
2oz (50g) Cheddar cheese
¼ pint (150ml) water
3oz (75g) margarine
2½oz (65g) brown flour
2 (size 4) eggs
1oz (25g) wholemeal flour
¼ pint (150ml) milk
¼ level tsp salt
⅛ level tsp dry mustard
pepper
2 level tbsps finely chopped parsley

1. Wet a baking tray. Preheat oven 200°C (400°F), gas 6.

2. Wash, dry, halve and thinly slice mushrooms. Peel and chop onion very finely. Grate cheese.

3. Place water and 2oz (50g) margarine in a pan, allow margarine to melt, bring to the boil and stir in brown flour all at once. Beat vigorously until paste leaves sides of pan. Cool slightly. Lightly whisk eggs, gradually add to flour mixture, beating well after each addition, until mixture forms soft peaks.

4. Spoon eight rounds on to prepared baking sheet. Bake for 30 minutes until puffy, crisp and golden. Remove from oven and slit half way through horizontally. Reduce oven temperature to 180°C (350°F), gas 4.

5. Melt remaining margarine, add mushrooms and onion and fry for 4 minutes. Stir in wholemeal flour and cook for 1-2 minutes. Blend in milk, bring to the boil and add salt, mustard and pepper. Simmer for 2-3 minutes. Remove from heat and stir in grated cheese and parsley.

6. Spoon sauce into choux buns and return to oven for 5 minutes.

Parsnip and Madeira Soufflé

Serves 6

Puréed parsnips, flavoured with Madeira, make a beautifully light soufflé. Serve straight from the oven with steamed French beans and sautéd grated carrot.

1¼lbs (600g) parsnips
½ level tsp salt
4 (size 3) eggs
3 tbsps Madeira
1 level tsp salt
pepper

1. Grease a 2½ pint (1.5 litre) soufflé dish. Preheat oven 190°C (375°F), gas 5.

2. Peel parsnips and slice into chunks. Place in a pan with water to cover and salt. Bring to the boil, cover, and simmer for 15 minutes. Drain.

3. Separate eggs. Place yolks in blender/processor with parsnips, Madeira, salt and pepper. Liquidise until smooth.

4. Stiffly whisk egg whites. Fold into parsnip purée. Pour into prepared dish and bake for 40-45 minutes until puffy and golden. Serve at once.

Buckwheat Peppers

Serves 4

Puffy red and green peppers, filled with nutty buckwheat, Brazils, mushrooms, sweetcorn and herbs make a delightfully colourful course without need for accompanying vegetables.

2 medium red peppers, approximate weight,
* 5oz (150g) each*
2 medium green peppers, approximate weight,
* 5oz (150g) each*
2oz (50g) onion
1oz (25g) Brazil nuts
2oz (50g) flat mushrooms
1 tbsp vegetable oil
2oz (50g) buckwheat
3oz (75g) sweetcorn kernels
2 level tbsps finely chopped parsley
½ level tsp finely chopped rosemary
¼ level tsp salt
½ pint (300ml) tomato juice
¼ pint (150ml) water
2 level tsps cornflour
⅛ level tsp salt
pepper

1. Wipe peppers. Slice off tops and remove pith and seeds. Peel and finely chop onion. Thinly slice Brazils. Wash, dry and finely chop mushrooms.

2. Heat oil. Add onion and fry for 8-10 minutes until golden. Add Brazils and buckwheat. Fry for a further 5 minutes.

3. Stir in mushrooms, sweetcorn, parsley, rosemary and seasonings. Pile mixture into pepper shells. Replace lids and stand in a closely fitting pan. Pour in tomato juice and water. Bring to the boil, cover, and simmer for 55-60 minutes.

4. Carefully lift peppers out of cooking liquid and keep warm in a serving dish. Blend cornflour with 2 tablespoons tomato stock. Add to pan with seasonings and simmer for 2-3 minutes. Hand sauce round with peppers.

Spicy Plantain with Green Pasta

Serves 4

Use green or ripe plantains, depending on how sweet you like them. Surrounded by spinach tagliatelle, this makes a delicious dish.

1lb (450g) tomatoes
1 clove garlic
¼ pint (150ml) water
2 tbsps vegetable oil
1 tbsp malt vinegar
finely grated peel and juice of 1 lime
¼ level tsp salt
2lbs (900g) plantains
8oz (225g) green tagliatelle

1. Skin and roughly chop tomatoes. Peel and crush garlic. Place in a pan with tomato, water, oil, vinegar, lime peel and juice and salt. Bring to the boil, cover, and simmer for 30 minutes.

2. Trim ends from plantains. Make a slit down both sides of skins. Cook, covered, in a large pan of boiling water, for 15 minutes. Drain.

3. Peel plantains and slice, diagonally, into ½" (12.5mm) thick ovals.

4. Add plantain to sauce and simmer, covered, for a further 10 minutes.

5. Cook tagliatelle in a pan of boiling salted water for 5-6 minutes. Drain well.

6. Arrange tagliatelle around edge of a warmed serving plate. Spoon plantain sauce into centre and serve.

Ratatouille Spiral Crumb

Serves 6

Wholewheat pasta spirals, stirred into a mélange of vegetables, and sprinkled with a light topping of cheese and breadcrumbs, makes an inexpensive lunchtime or evening meal. Serve on its own, or with finger carrots and a leafy green vegetable.

6oz (175g) onion
1 clove garlic
1lb (450g) courgettes
1lb (450g) aubergines
12oz (350g) tomatoes
4oz (125g) green pepper
1 tbsp vegetable oil
1 level tsp soft brown sugar
1 level tsp salt
pepper
4oz (125g) wholewheat pasta spirals
4oz (125g) Cheddar cheese
4oz (125g) wholemeal breadcrumbs

1. Lightly grease a 12″ (30cm) oval dish.

2. Peel and finely chop onion. Peel and crush garlic. Wipe, top and tail courgette, slice thinly. Wipe aubergine, remove stalk and slice thinly. Skin tomatoes and chop roughly. Wipe pepper, remove stalk and seeds, slice thinly.

3. Heat oil. Add onion and garlic and fry for 3-4 minutes. Add vegetables, sugar, salt and pepper. Bring to the boil, cover, and simmer for 45 minutes. Remove lid for last 15 minutes of cooking.

4. Cook pasta in plenty of boiling salted water for 10 minutes. Drain well and stir into ratatouille mixture. Pour into prepared dish.

5. Preheat grill on high. Grate cheese and mix with breadcrumbs. Sprinkle over ratatouille and grill for 3-4 minutes until cheese melts and breadcrumbs turn golden.

Root Rösti

Serves 4

Serve this flat vegetable cake during the winter months when root vegetables are good value for money and at their best. Accompany with a velvety onion sauce made with 12oz (350g) peeled and quartered onions, ½ pint (300ml) milk, a bayleaf, ¼ level teaspoon salt and pepper. Place all ingredients in a pan, bring to the boil, cover, and simmer for 30 minutes. Allow to cool slightly before liquidising in blender/processor.

12oz (350g) medium sized potatoes
12oz (350g) carrots
8oz (225g) turnips
1 (size 3) egg
¼ level tsp salt
⅛ level tsp ground mace
pepper
4 tsps vegetable oil

1. Peel potatoes, carrots and turnips. Leave whole, place in a pan with water to cover. Bring to the boil, cover, and simmer for 15 minutes. Drain.

2. Grate vegetables. Lightly beat egg and stir into vegetables with salt, mace and pepper.

3. Heat 3 teaspoons of oil in a frying pan with a 9" (23cm) diameter base. Spread vegetable mixture over base. Fry over a medium heat for 10 minutes.

4. Preheat grill on high. Sprinkle cake with remaining oil and grill for 6 minutes until golden. Serve at once with onion sauce.

Spinach and Cottage Cheese Slice

Serves 6

Here, layers of wholemeal pastry divide the subtly flavoured and colourful filling of spinach and cottage cheese. Assemble a couple of hours in advance so that the filling has time to soften the pastry slightly, and serve cold with a tomato and cucumber salad.

1lb (450g) spinach
¼ level tsp nutmeg
¼ level tsp salt
8oz (225g) wholemeal flour
¼ level tsp dry mustard
¼ level tsp salt
¼ level tsp paprika
2oz (50g) vegetable fat
2oz (50g) margarine
2-3 tbsps cold water
1 (size 4) egg
1 level tbsp sesame seeds
12oz (350g) cottage cheese

1. Preheat oven 220°C (425°F), gas 7.

2. Wash spinach in several changes of cold water. Drain and place in a large saucepan with nutmeg and salt. Cover, and cook for 6-7 minutes until leaves are limp.

3. Drain well, trim off any tough stalks and chop finely.

4. Sift flour, mustard, salt and paprika into a bowl. Rub in fat. Mix to a stiff dough with water, turn out onto a lightly floured surface and knead until smooth.

5. Roll out pastry into a 12" × 9" (30cm × 23cm) rectangle. Lift onto a baking sheet. Mark into three 9" × 4" (23cm × 10cm) strips. Brush one rectangle with beaten egg and sprinkle with sesame seeds. Bake for 15 minutes. Cut all the way through pastry marks and leave on tray until cold.

6. Stir cottage cheese into spinach.

7. Lay one strip of pastry on a serving plate. Smooth half spinach mixture over top. Repeat layers finishing with sesame seed strip.

Brussels Flan

Serves 6

It is well known that the flavours of sprouts and chestnuts complement each other. Here they are used as the basis for a savoury flan. Use fresh chestnuts when

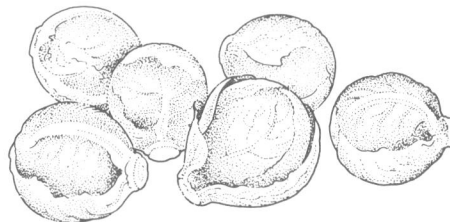

possible, alternatively, 4oz (125g) dried chestnuts, soaked overnight in 1 pint (600ml) boiling water, drained and simmered for 25-30 minutes, or until tender, may be substituted.

10oz (275g) sweet chestnuts
8oz (225g) Brussels sprouts
6oz (175g) wholemeal flour
¾ level tsp salt
1½oz (40g) vegetable fat
1½oz (40g) margarine
approximately 2 tbsps cold water
8fl oz (225ml) milk
3 (size 3) eggs
⅛ level tsp nutmeg

1. Preheat oven 220°C (425°F), gas 7.

2. Make a small slit in the rounded side of each chestnut shell. Drop into boiling water and simmer for 5 minutes. Drain, and while still hot, remove shell and scrape off inner skin. Remove outer leaves from sprouts, score stems with a cross.

3. Simmer chestnuts, covered, in a little water, for about 25 minutes, or until tender. Add sprouts 8 minutes before the end of cooking. Drain, and halve sprouts lengthways.

4. Place flour and ½ level teaspoon salt in a bowl. Rub in fat and mix to a stiff dough with water. Turn out onto a lightly floured surface and knead until smooth. Roll out thinly and use to line a 9″ (23cm) flan dish. Line with foil and bake blind for 15 minutes, removing foil after 10 minutes. Reduce oven temperature to 200°C (400°F), gas 6.

5. Scatter chestnuts and sprouts over pastry case. Lightly whisk together milk, eggs, remaining salt and nutmeg. Pour over vegetables and bake for 30 minutes until filling is golden and set.

Vegetables with Bulghur

Serves 6-8

A nutritious meal, combining a wealth of different vegetables.

4oz (125g) onion
6oz (175g) courgettes
6oz (175g) cauliflower
4oz (125g) red pepper
4oz (125g) mange-tout
2 tbsps vegetable oil
1oz (25g) pine kernels
2 level tbsps sunflower seeds
8oz (225g) bulghur
11½ fl oz (330ml) can vegetable and tomato juice
¾ level tsp salt
pepper

1. Peel and thinly slice onions into rings. Wipe, top and tail courgettes and slice thinly. Cut cauliflower into tiny florets. Wipe pepper, remove stalk and seeds, slice thinly. Remove stalks from mange-tout.

2. Heat 1 tablespoon oil. Add onion, pine kernels and sunflower seeds. Cook for 8-10 minutes, until the onion is golden.

3. Stir in courgettes, cauliflower, pepper and mange-tout. Add remaining oil, cover, and cook for 15 minutes, without browning. Shake pan occasionally.

4. Rinse bulghur, stir into vegetables. Make vegetable and tomato juice up to ¾ pint (450ml) with water. Add to pan with salt and pepper. Bring to the boil, cover, and cook for 8 minutes, or until the liquid is absorbed and bulghur cooked.

Cornish Vegetable Pasties

Serves 6

Golden cheese pastry envelopes a selection of diced vegetables, which may be varied according to seasonal availability. Alternatively, a mixture of fresh and thawed frozen vegetables, as is used here, may be incorporated. These pasties are equally good hot or cold.

2oz (50g) onion
2oz (50g) potato
2oz (50g) carrot
2oz (50g) turnip
2oz (50g) frozen peas, thawed
1 tbsp vegetable stock
½ level tsp salt
pepper
2oz (50g) Cheddar cheese
8oz (225g) wholemeal flour
1 level tsp baking powder
1 level tsp dry mustard
2oz (50g) vegetable fat
2oz (50g) margarine
2-3 tbsps cold water
milk for brushing

1. Lightly grease a baking sheet. Preheat oven 220°C (425°F), gas 7.

2. Peel and dice onion, potato, carrot and turnip into ¼″ (6mm) cubes. Place in a bowl with peas, stock, ¼ teaspoon salt and pepper. Mix well.

3. Grate cheese. Mix flour, baking powder, mustard and remaining salt in a bowl. Rub in fat, toss in cheese, and mix to a stiff dough with water. Turn out onto a lightly floured surface and knead until smooth.

4. Roll out dough thinly and cut 6 × 5″ (12cm) circles. Place a little vegetable mixture in the centre of each circle. Brush edges with milk. Fold pastry to form a turnover. Stand upright, so that the sealed edge is facing upwards, and crinkle to seal edges.

5. Place pasties on prepared tray. Brush with milk and bake for 10 minutes. Reduce temperature to 180°C (350°F), gas 4, and bake for a further 30 minutes. Either serve at once or transfer onto a wire rack to cool.

Vegetable Curry

Serves 6

Make this to your own taste, varying the assortment of vegetables at will, and serve with boiled brown rice. The vegetables look especially attractive when sliced diagonally.

4oz (125g) onion
½oz (15g) fresh root ginger
8oz (225g) Jerusalem artichokes
1 tsp lemon juice
12oz (350g) tomatoes
8oz (225g) courgettes
8oz (225g) carrots
8oz (225g) cauliflower florets
6oz (175g) okra
4oz (125g) celery
2 tbsps vegetable oil
5 level tsps Madras curry powder
¾ pint (450ml) water
2 level tbsps mango chutney
seeds of 6 green cardamom pods
2 level tbsps finely chopped coriander
1 level tbsp tomato purée
1½ level tsps salt
1 level tbsp cornflour

1. Peel and finely chop onion. Peel and finely chop ginger. Peel artichokes and dice into ½″ (12.5mm) cubes. Place in water to cover, with lemon juice. Skin and dice tomatoes into ½″ (12.5mm) cubes. Wipe courgettes, remove stem and slice fairly thinly. Peel and thinly slice carrots. Wash and drain cauliflower. Wash and dry okra, slice off stem and cut into ½″ (12.5mm) lengths. Wash and dry celery. Slice thinly.

2. Heat oil. Add onion and curry powder. Fry for 8-10 minutes until brown. Stir in ginger and vegetables, cover, and sauté for 10 minutes, without browning. Shake pan occasionally.

3. Stir in water, chutney, cardamom seeds, coriander, tomato purée and salt. Bring to the boil, cover, and simmer for 30 minutes.

4. Blend cornflour with 1 tablespoon water. Stir into curry and simmer for 2-3 minutes.

Granary Vegetable Crumble

Serves 6

A combination of nuts and granary flour provides a crunchy topping for the medley of fresh vegetables. This is an ideal way to use up left over cooked vegetables, the kind used may be varied in order to take full advantage of seasonal produce. Serve with a leafy green vegetable.

8oz (225g) carrots
4oz (125g) runner beans
6oz (175g) onion
4oz (125g) button mushrooms
8oz (225g) tomatoes
1 level tsp salt
4oz (125g) margarine
1oz (25g) wholemeal flour
¼ pint (150ml) milk
pepper
3 level tbsps finely chopped parsley
6oz (175g) malted wheat flour
2oz (50g) chopped mixed nuts

1. Preheat oven 200°C (400°F), gas 6.

2. Peel and quarter carrots. Cut into ½″ (12.5mm) lengths. Wash, top and tail, and thinly slice beans. Peel and roughly chop onion. Wash, dry and quarter mushrooms. Skin and dice tomatoes into ¼″ (6mm) cubes.

3. Place carrots in a pan with ½ pint (300ml) cold water and ½ teaspoon salt. Bring to the boil, cover, and simmer for 15 minutes. Add beans, onion and mushrooms and continue to cook for a further 5 minutes. Drain well, and reserve stock.

4. Melt 1oz (25g) margarine, add flour and cook for 1-2 minutes. Gradually blend in milk and ¼ pint (150ml) of reserved vegetable stock. Simmer for 2-3 minutes. Season with pepper.

5. Stir in cooked vegetables, tomato and parsley. Pour into a 2¾ pint (1.65 litre) pie dish.

6. Sift flour and remaining salt into a bowl. Rub in remaining fat, stir in nuts. Sprinkle over vegetables and press down lightly with fingertips. Bake for 30 minutes until evenly browned.

Hungarian Vegetable Casserole

Serves 4

The vegetables' natural flavours are allowed to take the stage in this casserole. Serve with baked potatoes, split, and topped with soured cream and chives.

6oz (175g) onion
8oz (225g) carrots
8oz (225g) parsnips
8oz (225g) Primo cabbage
8oz (225g) green pepper
2 tbsps vegetable oil
3oz (75g) wholemeal flour
¾ pint (450ml) vegetable stock
2 level tsps caraway seeds
1 level tsp paprika
¾ level tsp salt
⅛ level tsp cayenne pepper
¾ level tsp baking powder
1 level tsp mixed herbs
1oz (25g) shredded beef suet
2 tbsps cold water

1. Peel and thinly slice onion. Peel carrots and parsnips. Roughly chop into ¾″ (2cm) wedges. Discard any discoloured cabbage leaves. Cut into ¼″ (6mm) wide strips. Wash and drain. Wipe pepper, remove stalk and seeds. Cut into thin strips.

2. Heat oil. Add onion and fry until brown. Stir in 1oz (25g) flour, and cook for 2-3 minutes.

3. Blend in stock, add vegetables, caraway seeds, paprika, ½ level teaspoon salt and cayenne. Bring to the boil, cover, and simmer for 15 minutes.

4. Place remaining flour and salt, baking powder, herbs and suet in a bowl. Mix well. Bind to a soft dough with water. Shape into 8 balls.

5. Drop balls into casserole, cover, and simmer for a further 15-20 minutes without removing the lid.

Vegetable Stir Fry

Serves 2

Stir frying brings out the best in vegetables by conserving their true colour and flavour. Vary those which you use according to season, cooking the harder vegetables first.

4oz (125g) cauliflower
2oz (50g) onion
4oz (125g) curly kale
4oz (125g) carrots
6oz (175g) tomatoes
2 tbsps vegetable oil
1 tsp soy sauce

1. Cut cauliflower into tiny florets. Peel and thinly slice onion into rings. Discard tough stalks from kale, wash, drain and shred. Peel carrots and continue peeling in one direction, into wafer thin strips. Skin tomatoes and dice into ¼″ (6mm) cubes.

2. Heat oil. Add cauliflower and onion. Fry for 3 minutes, stirring all the time. Add kale and carrots. Cook for 2 minutes.

3. Stir in tomatoes and soy sauce. Cook for 1 minute. Serve at once.

Oriental Vegetable Omelettes

Serves 4

Delicious as a light meal, be sure to avoid overcooking the vegetables so that they remain bright and crisp and retain as many of their vitamins and minerals as possible. To do so, prepare all ingredients before you start cooking.

1 clove garlic
½oz (15g) fresh root ginger
6oz (175g) courgettes
2oz (50g) spring onions
4oz (125g) green pepper
2oz (50g) flat mushrooms
2oz (50g) bean or soya sprouts
6oz (175g) tomatoes
1 tbsp vegetable oil
1 level tbsp sesame seeds
salt
pepper

Omelettes
1 tsp vegetable oil
8 (size 3) eggs
4 tsps cold water
salt
pepper

1. Peel and crush garlic and ginger. Wipe courgettes, top and tail and dice into ¼" (6mm) cubes. Trim onions and slice thinly. Wipe pepper, remove stalk and seeds and slice into thin strips. Wash, dry, halve and thinly slice mushrooms. Wash and drain beansprouts. Skin tomatoes and dice into ½" (12.5mm) cubes.

2. Heat oil. Add garlic, ginger and sesame seeds. Cook for 2-3 minutes.

3. Stir in courgette, onion and pepper. Cook, uncovered, for 2-3 minutes.

4. Stir in mushrooms, beansprouts and tomatoes. Season, cover, and simmer for 5 minutes.

5. Meanwhile, heat oil in a 7" (18cm) base omelette pan. Pour off any excess. Lightly whisk together 2 eggs and 1 teaspoon water. Season with salt and pepper. Pour mixture into a pan, and as egg begins to set around edge, fork it to the middle, tilting pan to allow uncooked egg to run to the edge. Cook for 1-2 minutes until omelette is brown underneath.

6. Slide cooked omelette onto a plate. Spread half with a quarter of the vegetable mixture, fold uncovered half over filling. Repeat with remaining eggs to make a total of 4 omelettes. Serve at once.

VEGETABLES AND FISH

Pizza Jacket Potatoes

Serves 4

Baked potatoes, Italian style.

2 × 8oz (225g) potatoes
6oz (175g) tomatoes
8 black olives
3oz (75g) Mozarella cheese
1¾oz (50g) can anchovy fillets
1oz (25g) margarine
½ level tsp basil
pepper

1. Preheat oven 200°C (400°F), gas 6.

2. Scrub potatoes well, prick all over with a fork, and bake towards top of oven for 1 hour.

3. Skin and finely chop tomatoes. Remove stones from olives and chop very finely. Thinly slice Mozarella. Drain anchovies.

4. Halve potatoes horizontally and scoop out insides. Mash well and beat in tomato, olives, margarine, basil and pepper.

5. Pile filling back into potato skins. Lay cheese over top and arrange anchovy strips diagonally across cheese.

6. Place potatoes on a baking tray, return to oven for a further 15-20 minutes, until cheese has melted.

Fennel and Fish Croquettes

Makes 14

Serve these tasty croquettes with fresh tomato sauce and a seasonal green vegetable.

8oz (225g) fennel
6oz (175g) cod fillets
5oz (150g) low fat soft cheese
2oz (50g) wholemeal breadcrumbs
1 (size 3) egg
½ level tsp salt
¼ level tsp basil
⅛ level tsp paprika
3oz (75g) medium oatmeal

1. Wipe fennel, trim and grate finely. Remove skin and bones from cod. Flake into small pieces. Place in blender with fennel, cheese, breadcrumbs, egg, salt, basil and paprika. Blend until smooth.

2. Take level tablespoonfuls of mixture and shape into 3″ (7.5cm) croquettes. (This makes about 14). Roll in oatmeal, cover, and chill for 1 hour.

3. Grease a grill pan. Preheat grill on high. Cook croquettes for 10 minutes, turning occasionally, until golden.

Vegetable Marinaded Cod

Serves 4

The hot vegetable marinade partly cooks the fish whilst flavouring it at the same time. Serve this Chinese style dish with brown rice and peas.

6oz (175g) Chinese leaves
4oz (125g) Jerusalem artichokes
1 tsp lemon juice
2oz (50g) red pepper
2oz (50g) spring onions
½oz (15g) fresh root ginger
1 clove garlic
½ pint (300ml) vegetable or fish stock
2 tbsps vegetable oil
1 level tbsp clear honey
1 tbsp lemon juice
1 tbsp soy sauce
4 × 4oz (125g) cod fillets
2 level tsps cornflour

1. Wash and dry Chinese leaves. Shred finely. Peel artichokes and slice into matchstick sized pieces. Drop into water with lemon juice. Wipe pepper. Remove stalk and seeds, slice as for artichokes. Trim and thinly slice spring onions. Peel and finely chop ginger. Peel and crush garlic.

2. Drain artichokes. Place in a pan with prepared vegetables, stock, oil, honey, lemon juice and soy sauce. Bring to the boil, cover, and simmer for 5 minutes.

3. Pour marinade over fish and leave for 15 minutes. Using a slotted spoon, remove fish. Baste with a little marinade and cook under a high grill for 3-4 minutes.

4. Blend cornflour with 1 tablespoon cold water. Stir

into marinade, bring back to the boil and simmer for 2-3 minutes. Spoon over fish and serve.

Summer Fish and Vegetable Casserole

Serves 8

A light summer casserole made from fresh seasonal vegetables. Accompany with boiled new potatoes.

1lb (450g) tomatoes
12oz (350g) runner beans
6oz (175g) green pepper
4oz (125g) onion
1lb (450g) cod fillets
2 tbsps vegetable oil
12oz (350g) sweetcorn kernels
3 level tbsps wholemeal flour
½ pint (300ml) dry white wine
¼ pint (150ml) water
bayleaf
1 level tsp basil
1½ level tsps salt
pepper

1. Preheat oven 170°C (325°F), gas 3.

2. Skin and roughly chop tomatoes. Wash, drain, top and tail beans and slice thinly. Wipe pepper. Remove stalk and seeds. Quarter and slice thinly. Peel and thinly slice onion into rings. Remove skin from fish and dice into ¾″ (2cm) cubes.

3. Heat oil. Add beans, pepper, onion and sweetcorn. Cover, and cook for 10 minutes, without browning. Shake pan occasionally.

4. Stir in flour and cook for 1-2 minutes. Add tomato, wine, water, bayleaf, basil, salt and pepper. Bring to the boil and stir in fish.

5. Pour into a 4½ pint (2.8 litre) casserole. Cover, and bake for 50-60 minutes. Remove bayleaf and serve.

Fish Pie with Kolocassi

Serves 4

Crisp wafers of kolocassi make an unusual topping for coley in caper and anchovy sauce. Serve with minted peas.

4oz (125g) dried butterbeans
1lb (450g) kolocassi
2oz (50g) Cheddar cheese
12oz (350g) coley steaks
4 tbsps milk
bayleaf
milk to make up to ¼ pint (150ml)
1oz (25g) margarine
1oz (25g) plain flour
2 level tsps chopped capers
1 tsp anchovy essence
¼ level tsp salt
pepper
½ tub cress

1. Soak butterbeans overnight in plenty of cold water. Drain. Place in a pan, cover with water, bring to the boil, cover, and simmer for about 1¼ hours, until tender. Drain.

2. Grease two baking trays. Preheat oven 240°C (475°F), gas 9.

3. Peel kolocassi and slice very thinly. Lay slices out on baking trays and cook for 15 minutes, until crisp and golden. Reduce oven temperature to 200°C (400°F), gas 6.

4. Grate cheese. Place coley, milk and bayleaf in a 1½ pint (900ml) pie dish, cover, and bake for 20 minutes.

5. Pour off cooking liquor and make up to ¼ pint (150ml) with milk. Flake fish. Melt margarine, stir in flour and cook for 1-2 minutes. Blend in liquor, bring to the boil, cover, and simmer for 2-3 minutes. Stir in capers, anchovy essence, salt and pepper.

6. Pour into pie dish. Arrange kolocassi slices on top in two layers. Sprinkle with grated cheese and return to oven for a further 15 minutes until golden. Serve garnished with cress.

Celeriac and Haddock Soufflé Pie

Serves 6

A special occasion fish pie. Serve this celeriac and potato topped golden haddock sauce with tender young peas.

1½lbs (700g) celeriac
1 tsp lemon juice
1lb (450g) potatoes
2oz (50g) onion
2 cloves
1lb (450g) smoked haddock fillets
½ pint (300ml) milk
¾ level tsp salt
2oz (50g) margarine
1oz (25g) plain flour
pepper
2 (size 3) eggs

1. Grease a 2¾ pint (1.65 litre) pie dish. Preheat oven 200°C (400°F), gas 6.

2. Thickly peel celeriac. Cut into wedges and place in a bowl of cold water to cover, with lemon juice. Peel potatoes, cut into wedges and add to celeriac.

3. Peel onion, stud with cloves and place in a pan with fish and milk. Bring to the boil, cover, and simmer for

10 minutes. Drain and reserve cooking liquor. Skin, bone and flake fish.

4. Drain celeriac and potato. Place in a pan with ½ teaspoon salt and water to cover, bring to the boil, cover, and simmer for 20 minutes. Drain.

5. Melt 1oz (25g) margarine. Add flour and cook for 1-2 minutes. Blend in ½ pint (300ml) reserved milk, bring to the boil, add flaked fish, remaining salt and pepper. Simmer for 2-3 minutes. Pour into prepared pie dish.

6. Separate eggs. Place yolks, celeriac, potatoes and remaining margarine in blender/processor. Liquidise until smooth. Stiffly whisk whites and fold into purée. Spread over fish and bake for 30 minutes until puffy and golden.

Swiss Chard, Haddock and Mushroom Roulade

Serves 6

Definitely one for the dinner party! Grilled tomatoes and steamed French beans make a light accompaniment to this impressive, rich dish. If the roulade needs to be reheated this is best done wrapped in a piece of greased foil.

8oz (225g) smoked haddock
½ pint (300ml) milk
8oz (225g) Swiss chard
½ level tsp salt
2oz (50g) button mushrooms
4 (size 3) eggs
4oz (125g) wholemeal flour
¼ level tsp nutmeg
2oz (50g) margarine
2oz (50g) grated Parmesan cheese

1. Grease and line an 11″ × 8″ (23cm × 20cm) Swiss roll tin. Preheat oven 200°C (400°F), gas 6.

2. Place haddock in milk. Bring to the boil, cover, and simmer for 10-15 minutes. Drain and reserve milk. Remove skin and bones from fish, flake.

3. Wash and drain chard, trim stalks. Place in a large saucepan with ¼ teaspoon salt. Cover, and cook for 4 minutes until reduced. Drain well, chop finely and cool. Wash, dry and thinly slice mushrooms.

4. Whisk eggs until foamy and very thick. Fold in chard, 2oz (50g) flour, and nutmeg. Pour into Swiss roll tin, level surface, and bake for 10-12 minutes until just set.

5. Meanwhile, melt margarine, add mushrooms and fry for 2-3 minutes. Stir in remaining flour and cook for a further 1-2 minutes. Blend in reserved milk. Bring to the boil, add flaked haddock and remaining salt. Simmer for 2-3 minutes.

6. Dust a sheet of greaseproof paper with a thick layer of Parmesan. Turn roulade out onto cheese, carefully peel off paper. Spread with haddock filling, roll up from the long edge and serve immediately.

Kohlrabi, Corn and Haddock Stir Fry

Serves 4

A subtle blend of indistinguishable flavours, this dish goes well with creamed potatoes and young peas. If you cannot find oyster mushrooms use buttons instead.

1 clove garlic
¼oz (7g) fresh root ginger
1lb (450g) haddock fillets
12oz (350g) kohlrabi
6oz (175g) tomatoes
4oz (125g) oyster mushrooms
12oz (425g) can whole baby sweetcorn
2 tbsps vegetable oil
2 tsps soy sauce
1 tsp dry sherry
2 level tbsps finely chopped parsley

1. Peel and crush garlic and ginger. Skin haddock and remove any bones. Coarsely peel kohlrabi, grate. Peel and roughly chop tomatoes. Wash, drain, and halve mushrooms. Drain sweetcorn.

2. Heat oil in a large frying pan. Add garlic and ginger, cook for 1 minute. Stir in haddock and fry for 2 minutes, turning all the time.

3. Add kohlrabi, tomatoes, mushrooms, and sweetcorn. Simmer, uncovered, for 2-3 minutes, stirring continuously.

4. Stir in soy sauce and sherry. Sprinkle with parsley and serve at once.

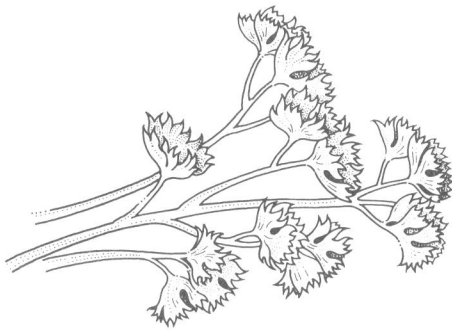

Herring with Sweetcorn Sauce

Serves 2

As an alternative use mackerel in place of herring for an equally pleasurable dish. Serve with sliced runner beans.

2 × 12oz (350g) herrings
1 small clove garlic
1oz (25g) wholemeal breadcrumbs
2 level tbsps finely chopped parsley
finely grated peel of ½ lemon
¼ level tsp salt
pepper
4 tsps milk
4 tbsps water
6oz (175g) sweetcorn kernels
¼ pint milk
1oz (25g) margarine
salt

1. Grease a long, shallow, ovenproof dish. Preheat oven 180°C (350°F), gas 4.

2. Make a slit down the stomach of the herrings. Wash out the insides, and pat dry. Peel and crush garlic.

3. Combine garlic, breadcrumbs, parsley, lemon peel and seasonings in a bowl. Mix to a moist consistency with milk.

4. Divide stuffing between fish and press into stomach cavity. Pour water into prepared dish. Lay herrings head to tail, cover loosely with foil and bake for 25-30 minutes until the flesh flakes.

5. Meanwhile, place sweetcorn, milk, margarine and seasonings in a small pan. Bring to the boil, cover, and simmer for 10 minutes. Cool slightly before puréeing in blender/processor. Return to pan and heat through. Serve at once with fish.

Mackerel and Watercress Slice

Serves 6

Cream cheese, watercress and tomato soused mackerel fillets, encased in crusty wholemeal bread, makes an original picnic or packed lunch filler.

2 level tsps dried yeast
1 level tsp soft brown sugar
¼ pint (150ml) warm water
8oz (225g) wholemeal flour
½ level tsp salt
½oz (15g) margarine
1 bunch watercress
2 × 4.41oz (125g) cans mackerel fillets in tomato sauce
8oz (227g) carton Quark cream cheese
¼ level tsp salt
1 (size 3) egg
1 level tbsp poppy seeds

1. Dissolve yeast and sugar in water. Leave to stand in a warm place for 15-20 minutes until frothy. Place flour and salt in a bowl. Rub in fat. Add yeast liquid and mix to a soft dough. Knead for 3-4 minutes until smooth. Place in a greased bowl, cover, and prove until doubled in size, about 1 hour.

2. Grease a baking sheet. Preheat oven 220°C (425°F), gas 7.

3. Wash and dry watercress. Trim and finely chop. Mash mackerel fillets in sauce. Beat cheese until smooth and stir in watercress, mackerel and salt.

4. Roll out on a lightly floured surface into 12″ × 8″ (30cm × 20cm) rectangle. Place mackerel mixture down the length of one half. Lightly beat egg and use to brush edges. Fold dough over to form a parcel, seal edges and lift onto prepared tray. Cover, and leave to prove in a warm place for about 45 minutes.

5. Make five slits in dough, brush with beaten egg and sprinkle with poppy seeds. Bake towards top of oven for 25 minutes. Serve hot, or cool on a wire rack.

Endive and Smoked Mackerel Mousse

Serves 10

Bitter endive leaves counteract the richness of mackerel. Serve with boiled new potatoes and a purée of fresh tomatoes.

1lb (450g) Batavian endive
12oz (350g) smoked mackerel fillets
0.4oz (11g) packet gelatine
½ pint (300ml) vegetable or fish stock
1oz (25g) margarine
1 tsp lemon juice
¼ pint (150ml) whipping cream
slices of lemon and endive leaves to garnish

1. Wash and drain endive. Remove skin from mackerel and flake.

2. Dissolve gelatine in stock. Allow to cool, but not set.

3. Place margarine in a pan with endive, cover, and cook for 10 minutes until wilted. Liquidise in blender/processor to a rough purée. Cool.

4. Mix together flaked fish and endive purée. Stir in gelatine mixture and lemon juice.

5. Stiffly whip cream and fold into mixture. Pour into a wetted 2½ pint (1.5 litre) soufflé dish. Refrigerate until set.

6. Unmould and serve garnished with slices of lemon and endive leaves.

Steamed Monkfish with Courgettes

Serves 4

Fleshy monkfish, seasoned with dill, steamed on a bed of young courgettes, is delicious served with brown rice.

4oz (125g) onion
12oz (350g) tomatoes
1 tsp vegetable oil
1 level tsp dill
4 tbsps dry white wine
1 tsp lemon juice
½ level tsp salt
pepper
1lb (450g) baby courgettes
1lb (450g) monkfish
1 level tsp cornflour

1. Peel and finely chop onion. Skin and roughly chop tomatoes. Heat oil, add onion and fry for 2-3 minutes. Stir in tomato, dill, wine, lemon juice and seasonings. Bring to the boil, cover, and simmer for 15 minutes.

2. Meanwhile, wipe, top and tail courgettes and halve lengthways. Remove skin and bones from fish, cut into ¾″ (2cm) chunks.

3. Lay courgettes, cut side down, on tomato mixture. Scatter monkfish over courgettes, cover, and simmer for a further 20 minutes.

4. Using a slotted spoon, transfer vegetables and fish onto a warmed serving plate. Blend cornflour with 1 tablespoon of the pan juices, stir into pan and simmer for 2-3 minutes. Adjust seasoning and pour over vegetables and fish.

Crunchy Topped Vegetable and Fish Parcels

Serves 4

Whole fish, braised with courgettes, mushrooms, onion, pepper and a little white wine, make a light summer dish, delicious served with minted new potatoes.

4 × 8-10oz (225-275g) grey or red mullet
1 clove garlic
12oz (350g) courgettes
4oz (125g) mushrooms
1 onion
1 red pepper
1oz (25g) margarine
1 tsp mixed herbs
salt
pepper
4 tbsps dry white wine
1oz (25g) wholemeal breadcrumbs

1. Preheat oven 190°C (375°F), gas 5.

2. Make a slit down the stomach of the mullet. Wash out the insides and pat dry. Snip off fins.

3. Peel and crush garlic. Wash, dry and thinly slice courgettes and mushrooms. Peel and thinly slice onion. Wipe pepper, remove stalk and seeds, slice thinly.

4. Melt margarine. Add vegetables, herbs, salt and pepper. Sauté for 5 minutes.

5. Place fish on individual pieces of foil, surround with vegetables, sprinkle 1 tablespoon of wine over each fish and fold over foil to seal parcels.

6. Place parcels on a baking tray and bake in oven for 30 minutes. Open out parcels and sprinkle breadcrumbs over fish. Bake for a further 10 minutes until breadcrumbs are crisp.

Fennel with Plaice in Pernod and Orange Sauce

Serves 4

Pernod enhances fennel's delicate aniseed flavour and is here blended into a creamy coating sauce for the fish and vegetable. Garnish with chopped parsley and a twist of orange, and serve with baked tomato slices and boiled new potatoes, tossed in parsley.

1lb (450g) fennel
1oz (25g) shallots
1 medium orange
4 plaice fillets, approximate weight 1lb (450g)
½ pint (300ml) milk
3 sprigs of parsley
½ level tsp salt
⅛ level tsp dry mustard
pepper
milk to make up to ½ pint (300ml)
1oz (25g) margarine
1oz (25g) plain flour
1tbsp Pernod
slice of orange

1. Trim stalks and slice base off fennel. Cut into ¼″ (6mm) wide rings. Wash and drain. Peel and finely chop shallots. Finely grate orange peel. Segment flesh. Halve each plaice fillet lengthways. Skin.

2. Place fennel in a pan with shallots, orange peel, milk, 1 sprig of parsley, salt, mustard and pepper. Bring to the boil, cover, and simmer for 10 minutes.

3. Place an orange segment in the centre of each fillet, roll up.

4. Place fish rolls on top of fennel. Cook, covered, for a further 10-15 minutes.

5. Using a slotted spoon, lift fennel into a shallow serving dish. Arrange fish on top. Keep warm.

6. Strain cooking liquor, make up to ½ pint (300ml) with milk, if necessary. Melt margarine, add flour and cook for 1-2 minutes. Gradually blend in liquor. Bring to the boil, add Pernod, and simmer for 2-3 minutes. Spoon over fish. Garnish with remaining parsley and a twist of orange.

Vegetable and Prawn Pilaff

Serves 4-6

Here the blended flavours of onion, fennel, pepper, tomato and mushrooms, provide a superb match for the prawns. Serve with a sprinkling of basil.

6oz (175g) onion
12oz (350g) fennel
6oz (175g) green pepper
8oz (225g) brown rice
12oz (350g) tomatoes
6oz (175g) button mushrooms
2 tbsps vegetable oil
¾ pint (450ml) vegetable or fish stock
1 level tsp basil
¼ level tsp salt

pepper
8oz (225g) shelled prawns
4 tbsps dry vermouth
basil to garnish

1. Peel and thinly slice onion into rings. Slice stalks and base from fennel. Thinly slice into rings. Wipe pepper, remove stalk and seeds. Dice in ½″ (12.5mm) cubes. Wash and drain rice. Skin and roughly chop tomatoes. Wash, dry and quarter mushrooms.

2. Heat oil in a large frying pan. Add onion and cook for 2-3 minutes. Stir in fennel and pepper. Cook for a further 2-3 minutes. Add rice and cook for 3-4 minutes.

3. Stir in tomato, mushrooms, half the stock, basil, salt and pepper. Bring to the boil, cover, and simmer for 45 minutes, gradually blending in stock.

4. Add prawns and vermouth, cover, and simmer for a further 15-20 minutes, or until all the liquid is absorbed. Stir occasionally.

5. Serve sprinkled with basil.

Salmon and Salsify Pie

Serves 4

Salmon and salsify, wrapped in flaky brown pastry, and served with fresh peas, is suitable for both special and informal occasions.

4oz (125g) brown flour
¼ level tsp salt
1½oz (40g) vegetable fat
1½oz (40g) margarine
4 tbsps cold water
1¼ tsps lemon juice
6oz (175g) salsify
7½oz (212g) can pink salmon

1 (size 3) hard boiled egg
½oz (15g) margarine
½oz (15g) plain flour
¼ pint (150ml) milk
salt
pepper
1 (size 4) egg

1. Place brown flour and salt in a bowl. Soften fat and rub in a quarter. Mix to a soft dough with water and ¼ teaspoon lemon juice. Roll into a rectangle and spread top two thirds with another quarter of fat. Fold bottom third of dough up and top third down. Seal edges, give a half turn and continue procedure until all the fat is used up. Wrap and refrigerate for at least 30 minutes.

2. Wet a baking sheet. Preheat oven 200°C (400°F), gas 6.

3. Scrub and peel salsify. Drop into a bowl of cold water with remaining lemon juice. Cook, covered, in boiling water for 20 minutes. Drain.

4. Drain salmon. Remove skin and bones. Flake. Peel and roughly chop hard boiled egg.

5. Melt margarine. Add flour and cook for 1-2 minutes. Blend in milk, bring to the boil and simmer for 2-3 minutes. Season with salt and pepper. Stir in salsify, salmon and chopped egg.

6. Roll out pastry into a 10″ (25cm) square. Place filling in a block in centre. Lightly beat egg. Brush edges of pastry with a little. Draw each corner up to meet in the centre. Seal edges and flute. Brush with egg and bake, towards top of oven, for 30 minutes.

Rainbow Trout with Sorrel Mayonnaise

Serves 4

If sorrel is not available then spinach is equally good. Hand the sauce round separately and serve with boiled potatoes and sautéd grated carrot.

1lb (450g) sorrel
½oz (15g) margarine
1 (size 3) hard boiled egg
¼ pint (150ml) mayonnaise
⅛ level tsp salt
pepper
1oz (25g) flaked almonds
4 × 8oz (225g) rainbow trout
vegetable oil for brushing

1. Wash sorrel in several changes of cold water. Drain and place in a large saucepan with margarine. Cover, and cook for 6-7 minutes until leaves are limp. Drain well and cool.

2. Place sorrel in blender/processor and liquidise until smooth. Shell and roughly chop egg. Add to sorrel with mayonnaise, salt and pepper. Blend until smooth. Cover, and chill.

3. Preheat grill on medium. Toast almonds until golden.

4. Make a slit down the stomach of the trout. Wash out the insides, and pat dry. Remove fins and brush with oil. Place under grill and cook for 10-15 minutes, turning once.

5. Place fish on a warmed serving dish. Sprinkle with almonds and serve with sorrel mayonnaise.

Chow Chow Boats

Serves 4

A pungent curried tuna topping combines well with the delicate flavour of chow chows. Accompany with grilled tomatoes and brown rice.

2 chow chows, approximate weight 10oz (275g) each
2oz (50g) onion
7oz (198g) can tuna in oil
2 level tsps Madras curry powder
1oz (25g) plain flour
¼ pint (150ml) milk
1 level tsp tomato purée
½ tsp lemon juice
½ level tsp salt
⅛ level tsp paprika

1. Grease a shallow ovenproof dish. Preheat oven 200°C (400°F), gas 6.

2. Place chow chows in boiling water and simmer, covered, for 30 minutes.

3. Peel and finely chop onion. Drain tuna, reserve oil and flake. Heat 2 tablespoons of the fish oil, add onion and curry powder, fry for about 10 minutes, or until the onion is golden brown.

4. Stir in flour and cook for 1-2 minutes. Blend in milk, bring to the boil, add flaked tuna, tomato purée, lemon juice, salt and paprika. Simmer for 2-3 minutes.

5. Drain chow chows. Halve, remove flat seeds, chop them finely and add to tuna sauce.

6. Divide sauce between chows and spread over cut side. Place in prepared dish, cover with a piece of foil and bake for 25 minutes.

VEGETABLES AND MEAT

Dudi with Beef Sauce

Serves 4

These long, thin vegetables make an intriguingly shaped holder for the beef and tomato filling. Topped with grated cheese, they are best served with creamed potatoes and a purée of carrots.

4oz (125g) onion
12oz (350g) tomatoes
1lb (450g) lean minced beef
4 level tsps plain flour
2 tsps Worcestershire sauce
bayleaf
½ level tsp basil
½ level tsp salt
pepper
2 × 12oz (350g) dudies
6oz (175g) Edam cheese

1. Lightly grease a shallow, oval, ovenproof dish. Preheat oven 200°C (400°F), gas 6.

2. Peel and finely chop onion. Skin tomatoes and finely chop.

3. Rapidly brown mince in a pan over a moderate heat. Add onion and cook for 2-3 minutes. Stir in flour and cook for 1-2 minutes. Add tomatoes, Worcestershire sauce, bayleaf, basil, salt and pepper. Bring to the boil, cover, and simmer for 30 minutes, stirring occasionally. Remove bayleaf.

4. Peel dudies and halve lengthways. Scoop out pulp, leaving a ¼" (6mm) thick shell. Finely chop pulp and add to sauce. Spoon sauce into shells.

5. Stand shells in prepared dish with 3 tablespoons of water. Cover loosely with foil and bake for 40 minutes.

6. Grate cheese. Remove foil from dudies, sprinkle them with cheese, and return to oven to cook for a further 10 minutes.

Bean, Beef and Tomato Stew

Serves 6

A summer casserole making the most of seasonal runner beans and tomatoes. Serve with scrubbed and boiled new potatoes.

6oz (175g) onions
1½lbs (700g) braising steak
1lb (450g) runner beans
1lb (450g) tomatoes
3 tbsps vegetable oil
2 level tbsps wholemeal flour
½ pint (300ml) meat stock
½ level tsp salt
pepper

1. Preheat oven 170°C (325°F), gas 3.

2. Peel and thinly slice onions. Trim any excess fat from beef. Dice into 1" (2.5cm) cubes. Wash, drain, top and tail beans and slice thinly. Skin and roughly chop tomatoes.

3. Heat oil. Add onion and fry for 8-10 minutes until golden. Drain and place in a 3½ pint (2.1 litre) ovenproof casserole.

4. Add meat to saucepan and fry for 3-4 minutes until brown. Drain and add to onion. Sprinkle flour into pan. Cook 1-2 minutes. Blend in stock, bring to the boil and add beans, tomatoes and seasonings.

5. Stir vegetable mixture into onions and beef. Cover, and cook in centre of oven for 2-2½ hours.

Palm Heart Beef Olives

Serves 4

Accompany these palm hearts, rolled in lean slices of wafer thin beef, with baked potatoes, carrots and winter cabbage.

4 large, thin slices of good stewing steak,
  approximate weight 1lb (450g)
7¾oz (220g) can palm hearts
4oz (125g) onion
2 tbsps vegetable oil
2 level tbsps plain flour
¾ pint (450ml) meat stock
¼ level tsp salt
pepper

1. Preheat oven 160°C (325°F), gas 3.

2. Place meat between two pieces of greaseproof paper and hammer out with a rolling pin until very thin. Slice pieces into three strips.

3. Drain palm hearts and roll each in a piece of meat. Secure with cotton or fine string.

4. Peel and thinly slice onion. Heat oil. Add meat and fry for 2-3 minutes until brown. Drain and place in a 2½ pint (1.5 litre) casserole dish.

5. Add onion and fry for 8-10 minutes until golden. Stir in flour and cook until just brown. Blend in stock, bring to the boil, season with salt and pepper and pour into casserole.

6. Cook in oven for 1½-1¾ hours.

Japanese Style Salsify with Beef

Serves 4

Oyster sauce enhances salsify's distinguised flavour as well as adding an oriental touch to the dish. Be sure to use only prime braising steak since cooking time is short and poor quality meat will toughen. Serve on a bed of egg noodles.

8oz (225g) black salsify (scorzonera)
1 tsp lemon juice
2oz (50g) onion
1lb (450g) best braising steak
bunch of watercress
3 tbsps vegetable oil
3 level tbsps oyster sauce

1. Scrub, peel and wash salsify. Holding a sharp knife at an angle, shave off thin ovals of vegetable. Place in a bowl with lemon juice to prevent browning.

2. Peel and finely chop onion. Thinly slice beef in a similar way to salsify, making thin, long shavings. Wash, dry, and trim watercress. Roughly chop.

3. Heat oil until very hot. Drain salsify and add to pan with onion. Fry over a high heat for 2 minutes. Add meat and cook for a further 3 minutes, until browned.

4. Stir in watercress and oyster sauce, reduce heat and simmer for 1 minute. Serve at once.

Steak, Kidney and Shallot Pudding

Serves 8

Serve this winter pudding with sprouts, carrots and extra gravy.

1lb (450g) stewing steak
12oz (350g) small shallots or pickling onions
8oz (225g) ox kidney
3 level tbsps seasoned flour
12oz (350g) wholemeal flour
3 level tsps baking powder
6oz (175g) shredded suet
½ level tsp salt
16 tbsps cold water

1. Grease a 3 pint (1.8 litre) pudding basin.

2. Trim excess fat from steak. Dice into ½″ (12.5mm) cubes. Peel onions and leave whole. Remove core from kidneys. Dice into ½″ (12.5mm) cubes. Toss steak and kidney in seasoned flour.

3. Put a large saucepan, half filled with water, on to boil.

4. Place wholemeal flour, baking powder, suet and salt in a bowl. Mix well. Bind to an elastic dough with about 13 tablespoons water.

5. Roll out three quarters of the dough and use to line prepared pudding basin. Place meat and onions in basin with 3 tablespoons of water. Dampen edges. Roll out remaining pastry to form a lid. Place on top and seal well.

6. Cover with foil, secure with string or an elastic band. Steam, covered, in a pan of rapidly boiling water for 5 hours. Add more boiling water to pan when necessary, to prevent it from burning dry. Remove foil and serve with a napkin tied around the basin.

Lamb and Aubergine Filled Vine Parcels

Serves 8

Aubergines, vine leaves and lamb together conjure up pictures of Greek cuisine. Traditionally known as dolmades, these little parcels may be served, as they are in Greece, as appetisers, or a main course (allow four per person), with grilled tomatoes, sautéd cucumber slices and wholemeal rolls.

8oz (225g) packet of vine leaves
10oz (275g) aubergine
12oz (350g) neck of lamb fillet
1 clove garlic
2oz (50g) brown rice
1 level tbsp tomato purée
1 level tsp finely chopped rosemary
¼ level tsp salt
½ pint (300ml) meat stock

1. To remove excess salt from vine leaves, place in a bowl, cover with boiling water, and leave to stand for 20 minutes. Rinse with cold water and drain thoroughly.

2. Wipe aubergines, trim stalk and cook, whole, in boiling water for 20 minutes. Plunge into cold water to prevent further cooking. When cold, dice into ¼" (6mm) cubes.

3. Trim any excess fat from lamb. Mince. Peel and crush garlic. Place aubergine in a bowl with lamb, garlic, rice, tomato purée, rosemary and salt. Mix well.

4. Spread out leaves, stem side upwards. Place a heaped teaspoon of mixture in centre of each, near the stem end. Fold stem end, then both sides of the leaf, over filling. Roll up tightly. This makes about 34 dolmades.

5. Line the bottom of a large, shallow pan with remaining vine leaves, to prevent the meat parcels sticking. Arrange parcels in a single layer on top. Pour over stock.

6. Bring to the boil, cover, and simmer for 1 hour. Serve with pan juices.

Lamb Balls in Bean and Tomato Sauce

Serves 4

Serve these meat balls on a bed of wholewheat or spinach spaghetti, allowing 2oz (50g) per person.

4oz (125g) dried aduki beans
1lb (450g) neck of lamb fillet
1 clove garlic
4oz (125g) onion
1lb (450g) tomatoes
4oz (125g) wholemeal breadcrumbs
¾ level tsp salt
pepper
1 (size 3) egg
2 level tbsps wholemeal flour
1 tbsp vegetable oil
¾ pint (450ml) meat stock
2 level tbsps mango chutney
2 tsps white wine vinegar
2 level tsps cornflour

1. Soak aduki beans overnight in plenty of cold water. Place in a pan, cover with water, bring to the boil, cover, and simmer for 15 minutes. Drain.

2. Trim any excess fat from lamb. Mince. Peel and crush garlic. Peel and finely chop onion. Skin and roughly chop tomatoes.

3. Place mince, garlic, breadcrumbs, ¼ level teaspoon

salt and pepper in a bowl. Mix thoroughly. Lightly beat egg and use to bind mixture.

4. Divide into 16 and shape into 1½" (4cm) diameter balls. Roll in flour.

5. Heat oil. Add onion and fry for 3-4 minutes. Stir in tomato, stock, chutney, vinegar, remaining salt and aduki beans. Bring to the boil, drop in meat balls, cover, and simmer for 30 minutes.

6. Blend cornflour with 1 tablespoon cold water. Stir into pan and simmer for 2-3 minutes until thickened.

Liver and Artichoke Strogonoff
Serves 4

An unusual blend of flavours — serve with brown rice and purple sprouting broccoli.

8oz (225g) pigs' livers
½oz (15g) seasoned wholemeal flour
14oz (397g) can artichoke hearts
2oz (50g) onion
2oz (50g) green pepper
2oz (50g) red pepper
1oz (25g) margarine
5.29oz (150g) carton natural low fat yoghurt
⅛ level tsp salt
pepper

1. Wash and dry livers. Slice into 2" (5cm) strips. Toss in seasoned flour.

2. Drain artichoke hearts and quarter. Peel and finely chop onion. Wipe peppers. Remove stalks and seeds, slice thinly.

3. Melt margarine. Add onion and peppers, fry for 2-3 minutes. Add liver and artichoke hearts, fry for a further 4-5 minutes.

4. Stir in yoghurt and seasonings, heat through, without boiling, and serve at once.

Red Cabbage and Sausages Braised in Cider

Serves 4

Cider imparts a pleasantly sweet taste to the red cabbage, and pairs well with pork sausages to make an enjoyable everyday family dish. Serve with creamed potatoes and Brussels sprouts.

6oz (175g) onion
1lb (450g) red cabbage
1oz (25g) margarine
1oz (25g) plain flour
½ pint (300ml) cider
½ pint (300ml) meat stock
1 tbsp cider vinegar
1 level tsp salt
pepper
8oz (225g) skinless pork sausages

1. Preheat oven 160°C (325°F), gas 3.

2. Peel and finely chop onion. Finely shred red cabbage, wash and drain.

3. Melt margarine. Add onion and fry for 8-10 minutes until golden brown. Stir in flour and cook for 2-3 minutes. Blend in cider, stock and vinegar. Bring to the boil and season with salt and pepper.

4. Place red cabbage and sausages in a 3 pint (1.8 litre) ovenproof casserole. Pour over cider sauce, cover, and cook for 2 hours.

Hawaian Style Pork Roll

Serves 4

Full of Caribbean colour, tender pork fillet encasing a moist stuffing of crushed pineapple, spring onions, red pepper, celery, coconut, and glazed with a pepper and onion sauce, goes well with brown rice and petits pois.

2 × 8oz (225g) pork tenderloin fillets
13.3oz (376g) can crushed pineapple
4oz (125g) spring onions
4oz (125g) red pepper
2oz (50g) celery
2oz (50g) wholemeal breadcrumbs
1oz (25g) desiccated coconut
½ level tsp salt
¼ level tsp allspice
2 level tsps cornflour
1 tbsp malt vinegar

1. Grease a large piece of foil. Preheat oven, 200°C (400°F), gas 6.

2. Slit pork fillets horizontally, being careful not to slice all the way through. Open meat out and place between 2 sheets of greaseproof paper. Bang out with a rolling pin until thin.

3. Drain pineapple and reserve syrup. Trim onions, wash and thinly slice. Wipe pepper. Remove stalk and seeds. Chop finely. Wipe celery, trim and finely chop. Combine pineapple, 3oz (75g) onion, 2oz (50g) red pepper, celery, breadcrumbs, coconut, salt and allspice in a bowl.

4. Place fillets side by side, and overlapping by about ½″ (12.5mm), on a flat surface. Spoon stuffing mixture down the length and form into a log. Draw up meat over stuffing so as to encase the mixture. Tie securely with fine string or cotton. Tuck ends under and wrap loosely in foil. Place on a baking sheet. Bake for 50 minutes.

5. Measure ¼ pint (150ml) of reserved pineapple syrup. Blend cornflour with 1 tablespoon syrup. Place syrup in a small pan with vinegar, remaining onion and pepper. Bring to the boil, stir in cornflour and simmer for 5 minutes, stirring occasionally.

6. Remove pork roll from foil. Cut away string and place on a warmed serving plate. Coat with onion and pepper glaze, and hand round meat juices separately if wished.

Curried Kolocassi Pork Balls

Makes 8

Mildly flavoured with curry paste, kolocassi's slightly slippery texture makes it ideal for moulding into balls. Serve these rich, crisp sausagemeat 'eggs' with any green vegetable.

1lb (450g) kolocassi
1oz (25g) margarine
1 level tsp hot curry paste
¼ level tsp salt
1oz (25g) wholemeal flour
1¼lbs (600g) pork sausagemeat
2 (size 3) eggs
3oz (75g) wholemeal breadcrumbs

1. Peel kolocassi and slice thickly. Place in a pan of salted water. Bring to the boil, cover, and simmer for 20 minutes until tender.

2. Drain well and mash. Beat in margarine, curry paste and salt. Cool.

3. Lightly grease a baking tray. Preheat oven 200°C (400°F), gas 6.

4. Divide kolocassi mixture into eight and roll into 'egg shaped' ovals. Toss in flour.

5. Divide sausagemeat into eight. Press out thinly in palm of hand. Carefully mould round kolocassi.

6. Lightly beat eggs. Roll balls in egg and coat with breadcrumbs. Place on prepared tray and bake for 30 minutes until crisp and golden.

Leek and Ham Terrine

Serves 6-8

Creamy leek purée, layered with ham, slices into an inspiring cold terrine for buffet parties.

2lbs (900g) leeks
5fl oz (142ml) carton double cream
2 (size 3) eggs
⅛ level tsp nutmeg
5 thin slices cooked ham measuring 6½″ × 4″
  (17cm × 10cm)

1. Grease and line a 7½″ (19cm) long by 3½″ (9cm) wide, 2lb (900g) loaf tin with foil. Have ready a water bath with boiling water. Preheat oven 180°C (350°F), gas 4.

2. Trim leeks 1″ (2.5cm) above green stalk. Reserve a 1″ (2.5cm) length of stalk and slice, lengthwise, into julienne strips. Wash and drain leeks. Cook, covered, in boiling salted water for 15 minutes. Drain. Blanch julienne strips in boiling water for 30 seconds. Drain.

3. Purée cooked leeks until smooth. Blend in cream, eggs and nutmeg.

4. Lay two slices of ham over base and ends of tin. Pour in half the leek purée. Make a layer with ham, pour in remaining purée and lay remaining ham slices on top. Cover with foil.

5. Place tin in water bath. Bake for 1 hour. Pour off excess liquid. Weight down and leave overnight.

6. Unmould terrine onto a serving plate. Remove foil and garnish with julienne strips of leek before serving.

Sweet Potato, Pork and Apple Bake

Serves 6

Made in minutes using a food processor, this is equally good served hot with runner beans and steamed cauliflower in a walnut white sauce, or cold, having been baked in a greased 1lb (450g) loaf tin and allowed to cool before being cut into slices. Hand round a green salad and wedges of tomato separately.

8oz (225g) sweet potato
2oz (50g) onion
8oz (225g) cooking apples
1lb (450g) minced pork
2oz (50g) wholemeal breadcrumbs
¼ level tsp sage
¼ level tsp salt
pepper
1 (size 3) egg

1. Grease a 1½ pint (900ml) pie dish. Preheat oven 190°C (375°F), gas 5.

2. Peel and grate potato and onion. Peel, core and grate apples.

3. Place in a bowl with pork, breadcrumbs, sage, salt and pepper. Mix well. Lightly beat egg and stir in.

4. Spoon into prepared dish, level surface, and bake, uncovered, for 1 hour.

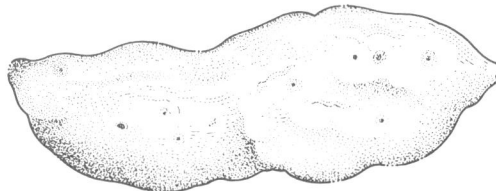

Yam and Ham Nests

Serves 4

Enjoyed by both adults and children, serve these nests with finger carrots and a green leafy vegetable.

1lb (450g) yam
4oz (125g) button mushrooms
4oz (125g) cooked lean ham
1½oz (40g) margarine
½oz (15g) plain flour
¼ pint (150ml) milk, plus 4 tbsps
¼ level tsp salt
pepper

1. Grease a baking tray. Preheat oven 180°C (350°F), gas 4.

2. Peel and thickly slice yam. Place in a pan of salted water to cover. Bring to the boil, cover, and simmer for 20 minutes until tender. Drain.

3. Wash, dry and thinly slice mushrooms. Dice ham into ¼″ (6mm) cubes.

4. Melt ½oz (15g) margarine. Add mushrooms and cook for 2-3 minutes. Stir in flour and cook for 1-2 minutes. Blend in ¼ pint (150ml) milk, bring to the boil and simmer for 2-3 minutes. Stir in ham, salt and pepper.

5. Mash yams. Beat in remaining margarine and milk. Divide into four and shape into 4″ (10cm) 'nests' on baking tray.

6. Pour mushroom and ham sauce into dip in centre of 'nests' and bake for 15 minutes.

Kidney, Shallot and Red Pepper Casserole

Serves 4

Kidneys — one of the most underrated foods — simmered with shallots and red pepper are suitable for the grandest or simplest occasions. Serve with creamed potatoes and sprouts.

1lb (450g) lambs' kidneys
4oz (125g) shallots
4oz (125g) red pepper
1oz (25g) margarine
½ pint (300ml) meat stock
bouquet garni
½ level tsp salt
pepper
4 medium slices wholemeal bread, approximate weight
   5oz (150g)
2 level tsps Meaux mustard

1. Wash, dry, halve, skin and core kidneys. Peel shallots. Wipe pepper, remove core and seeds, dice into ½″ (12.5mm) cubes.

2. Melt margarine. Add kidneys and cook for about 5 minutes, until browned. Stir in shallots, pepper, stock, bouquet garni and seasonings. Bring to the boil, cover, and simmer for 15 minutes.

3. Trim crusts from bread. Spread each slice with ½ level teaspoon mustard. Stir into kidneys, cover, and simmer for a further 15 minutes. Remove bouquet garni and serve.

VEGETABLES AND POULTRY

Chicken Liver and Aubergine Fans

Serves 4

Decorative aubergine fans, filled with a rich chicken liver mixture, topped with garlic cream sauce and showered with finely chopped parsley, makes an impressive dinner party dish. Accompany with a seasonal green vegetable, lightly cooked cabbage goes well, and boiled potatoes. A thin chicken flavoured gravy may be substituted for the garlic sauce if preferred.

12oz (350g) aubergine
8oz (225g) chicken livers
2oz (50g) shallots
4oz (125g) tomatoes
½oz (15g) margarine
2oz (50g) wholemeal breadcrumbs
1 level tbsp finely chopped parsley
½ level tsp salt
¼ level tsp mixed herbs
pepper

Garlic cream sauce
1 clove garlic
5fl oz (142ml) carton soured cream
2 tbsps milk
¼ level tsp salt
pepper
1 level tbsp finely chopped parsley

1. Preheat oven 200°C (400°F), gas 6.

2. Wipe aubergine. Remove stalk and halve lengthways. Place cut side down, and starting from the stalk end make an incision, ¼″ (6mm) from the top and cut down to the other end, ¼″ (6mm) from the edge. Repeat, slicing into 7-8 'tongues' which are attached at the top.

3. Wash, dry and finely chop chicken livers. Peel and finely chop shallots. Skin and roughly chop tomatoes.

4. Melt margarine. Fry livers for 3-4 minutes, until lightly browned. Stir in shallots, tomatoes, breadcrumbs, parsley, salt, herbs and pepper. Mix thoroughly.

5. Open out aubergines into a fan. Spread the surface of each slice with a little liver mixture. Place in a large ovenproof dish, cover with foil, and bake for 40 minutes.

6. To make garlic sauce, peel and crush garlic. Place in a small pan with cream and seasonings. Bring slowly to the boil and simmer, uncovered, for 2-3 minutes. Pour over aubergines just before serving. Sprinkle with chopped parsley.

83

Broccoli and Chicken Crêpes

Makes 8-10

Leftover chicken with freshly cooked broccoli, encased in wholemeal pancakes, and topped with a cream sauce makes a delicious dish. Serve with sautéd mushrooms and jacket potatoes.

8oz (225g) broccoli spears
8oz (225g) cooked chicken
4oz (125g) Cheddar cheese
4oz (125g) wholemeal flour
¾ level tsp salt
1 (size 3) egg
¼ pint (150ml) water
¼ pint (150ml) skimmed milk
1 tsp vegetable oil
2oz (50g) margarine
2oz (50g) plain flour
½ pint (300ml) milk
1 level tsp made mustard
½ level tsp paprika
5fl oz (142ml) carton soured cream
2 (size 3) egg yolks
2 tbsps dry vermouth

1. Grease a large ovenproof dish. Preheat oven 230°C (450°F), gas 8.

2. Wash and drain broccoli. Trim off any tough stems. Simmer, covered, in salted water, for 15-20 minutes. Drain and roughly chop. Dice chicken into ¼″ (6mm) cubes. Grate cheese.

3. Place flour and ½ level teaspoon salt in a bowl. Make a well in the centre and add egg and water. Mix to a smooth batter. Gradually whisk in milk.

4. Heat oil in a 7″ (18cm) diameter omelette pan. Pour off any excess. Spoon enough batter to just cover the base into pan, and cook for 1-2 minutes on each side until golden. This makes 8-10 pancakes.

5. Melt margarine, add flour and cook for 1-2 minutes. Blend in milk, bring to the boil and add remaining salt, mustard and paprika. Simmer for 2-3 minutes. Stir in broccoli, chicken and 2oz (50g) grated cheese.

6. Divide filling between pancakes, spooning into a line down the centre of each. Roll up, and arrange in prepared dish.

7. Lightly whisk together cream, egg yolks and vermouth. Pour over pancakes. Sprinkle with remaining cheese and bake towards top of oven for 15-20 minutes until golden.

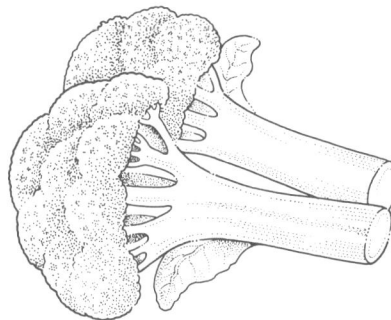

Celery and Chicken Ring with Mushroom Sauce

Serves 4

This crunchy celery and chicken ring goes well with sweetcorn, stir fried with red pepper. Spoon the mushroom sauce over the ring just before serving, or hand round separately.

2oz (50g) unsalted peanuts
8oz (225g) celery
5oz (150g) boned and skinned chicken breast
2oz (50g) onion
2oz (50g) margarine
3 level tbsps finely chopped parsley
2 (size 3) eggs
2oz (50g) wholemeal breadcrumbs
¼ level tsp salt
pepper

Mushroom sauce
2oz (50g) button mushrooms
½oz (15g) margarine
½oz (15g) plain flour
¼ pint (150ml) milk
salt
pepper

1. Grease a 2 pint (1.2 litre) ring mould. Preheat grill on high. Preheat oven 180°C (350°F), gas 4.

2. Roast peanuts for 2-3 minutes, rub between a teatowel to remove skins. Chop finely.

3. Wash and finely chop celery. Mince chicken. Peel and finely chop onion. Melt margarine. Place all ingredients in a bowl with peanuts, parsley, beaten eggs, breadcrumbs and seasoning. Mix well. Spoon into prepared mould, place on a baking sheet and cook for 35 minutes.

4. For the mushroom sauce, wash, dry and finely chop mushrooms. Melt margarine, add mushrooms and fry for 2-3 minutes. Stir in flour and cook for 1-2 minutes. Gradually blend in milk. Simmer for 2-3 minutes. Season to taste with salt and pepper.

5. Unmould celery and chicken ring. Serve with mushroom sauce.

Creole Chicken

Serves 4

Classically Mexican, serve this stew with sweetcorn and brown rice.

2oz (50g) onion
1 clove garlic
6oz (175g) tomatoes
4oz (125g) okra
3oz (75g) green pepper
1oz (25g) green chillies
2 tbsps vegetable oil
4 × 9oz (250g) chicken quarters
¼ pint (150ml) chicken stock
½ level tsp salt
¼ level tsp celery salt
¼ level tsp paprika
⅛ level tsp chilli powder
2 level tsps cornflour

1. Peel and finely chop onion. Peel and crush garlic. Skin and roughly chop tomatoes. Wash and dry okra. Remove stalk and slice into ¾" (2cm) lengths. Wipe pepper and chillies. Remove stalks and seeds. Quarter pepper lengthways, and slice across into ¼" (6mm) thick strips. Thinly slice chillies.

2. Heat oil. Add chicken quarters and fry for 6-8 minutes until both sides are brown. Using a slotted spoon remove from pan. Add onion and garlic. Cook for 2-3 minutes.

3. Return chicken pieces to pan with tomatoes, okra, pepper and chillies. Add stock and seasonings. Bring to the boil, cover, and simmer for 40-45 minutes.

4. Remove chicken pieces and keep hot on serving dish. Blend cornflour with 1 tablespoon water. Stir into vegetable mixture, bring to the boil and simmer for 2-3 minutes. Pour over chicken and serve.

Curried Carrot and Chicken

Serves 4

Carrots and butterbeans combine well in this curry, which is delicately flavoured with 'home-made' coconut milk. Serve on a bed of brown rice, cooked in boiling water, to which a little turmeric has been added.

4oz (125g) butterbeans
2oz (50g) desiccated coconut
4 × 9oz (350g) chicken quarters
1oz (25g) seasoned plain flour
4oz (125g) onion
12oz (350g) carrots
2 tbsps vegetable oil
1 level tbsp Madras curry powder
½ pint (300ml) chicken stock
2 level tbsps finely chopped coriander
1 level tsp salt
pepper

1. Soak butterbeans overnight in ¾ pint (450ml) cold water. Drain.

2. Pour ½ pint (300ml) boiling water onto coconut and leave to infuse for 10 minutes. Strain and reserve liquor.

3. Toss chicken quarters in seasoned flour. Peel and finely chop onion. Peel and slice carrots into ¼″ (6mm) rounds.

4. Heat oil. Add chicken and fry for 6-8 minutes until browned on both sides. Using a slotted spoon, remove from pan. Add onion and curry powder. Fry for 8-10 minutes until onion is golden. Add remaining seasoned flour and cook for 1-2 minutes. Blend in coconut milk and stock. Bring to the boil.

5. Add butterbeans, chicken, carrots, coriander and seasonings, cover, and simmer for 45 minutes, or until chicken is tender.

Green Omelettes with Chicken Paprika Filling

Serves 2

According to the time of year, spring greens, Brussels tops or cabbage may be substituted for spring cabbage.

8oz (225g) spring cabbage
2oz (50g) onion
6oz (175g) cooked chicken
2oz (50g) Cheddar cheese
1oz (25g) margarine
½oz (15g) plain flour
¼ pint (150ml) milk
¼ level tsp salt
¼ level tsp paprika
1 tsp vegetable oil
4 (size 3) eggs
2 tsps water

1. Remove tough stalks from cabbage. Finely shred, wash, and drain well. Peel and finely chop onion. Dice chicken into ¼″ (6mm) cubes. Grate cheese.

2. Melt ½oz (15g) margarine. Add cabbage and onion. Fry for 10 minutes, stirring occasionally.

3. Melt remaining margarine. Stir in flour and cook for 2-3 minutes. Blend in milk. Bring to the boil, add chicken and seasonings, simmer for 3-4 minutes. Remove from heat and stir in cheese. Cover.

4. Heat oil in a 7″ (18cm) omelette pan. Pour off any excess oil. Lightly whisk together 2 eggs and 1 teaspoon water. Season with salt and pepper to taste. Pour into pan, add half cabbage mixture, and as egg begins to set around edges fork it to the middle, tilting pan to allow uncooked egg to run to the edge. Cook for 1-2 minutes until omelette is brown underneath.

5. Slide omelette onto warm serving plate. Reheat

chicken filling. Spread half over omelette. Flip omelette over to make a semi-circle and serve at once. Repeat with remaining eggs.

Tropical Chicken and Eddoe Pie

Serves 4

Coconut and rum soused chicken, topped with creamed eddoe, speckled with spring onion, makes an unusual pie. Serve with peas.

1lb (450g) eddoes
2oz (50g) spring onions
6oz (175g) cooked chicken
3 level tbsps mayonnaise
2 tbsps milk
½oz (15g) desiccated coconut
2 tsps rum
1½oz (40g) margarine

1. Preheat oven 200°C (400°F), gas 6.

2. Peel eddoes and slice thickly. Place in a pan with salted water to cover. Bring to the boil, cover, and simmer for 20 minutes until tender. Drain.

3. Trim and thinly slice spring onions. Dice chicken into ½″ (12.5mm) cubes.

4. Mix together mayonnaise and milk. Blend in coconut and rum. Stir in chicken and spoon into a 1½ pint (900ml) pie dish.

5. Mash eddoes. Beat in spring onion and 1oz (25g) margarine. Spoon over chicken and level surface.

6. Melt remaining margarine and use to brush top of pie. Bake for 20 minutes. Brown under a high grill.

Golden Chicken with Salsify

Serves 4

Salsify has a velvety smooth texture which is complemented by serving it with wedges of crisp lettuce.

1lb (450g) salsify
1 tsp lemon juice
4 × 9oz (250g) chicken quarters
1 level tsp salt
bouquet garni
16fl oz (475ml) milk
2oz (50g) semolina
2 (size 3) eggs
2 level tbsps grated Parmesan cheese
1oz (25g) margarine
½ level tsp salt
pepper
sprig of parsley to garnish

1. Scrub and peel salsify. Cut into ½″ (12.5mm) lengths and place in a bowl of water with lemon juice to prevent browning.

2. Skin chicken and place in a pan with water to just cover. Add salt and bouquet garni. Bring to the boil, cover, and simmer for 45 minutes. Add salsify after 20 minutes.

3. Place milk and semolina in a pan. Bring to the boil and simmer for 4-5 minutes until thick, stirring continuously. Remove from heat.

4. Lightly beat eggs. Beat into semolina with Parmesan, margarine and seasonings. Return to heat, bring back to the boil and simmer for 2-3 minutes.

5. Drain chicken and arrange on a warmed serving dish, with salsify lengths in a row down either side. Pour over sauce and garnish with parsley.

Vegetable and Chicken Breadcrumb Flan

Serves 4

This combination of vegetables and chicken in a creamy sauce, encased in a crisp breadcrumb shell, makes a luxurious midday or evening meal.

2oz (50g) Cheddar cheese
4oz (125g) wholemeal breadcrumbs
2½oz (65g) margarine
1 level tsp tarragon
2oz (50g) celery
2oz (50g) red pepper
2oz (50g) flat mushrooms
4oz (125g) sweetcorn kernels
½oz (15g) plain flour
¼ pint (150ml) single cream
¼ level tsp salt
pepper
8oz (225g) cooked chicken

1. Lightly grease a 9″ (23cm) round of foil. Preheat oven 220°C (425°F), gas 7.

2. Finely grate cheese. Place breadcrumbs in a bowl, rub in 2oz (50g) margarine. Toss in cheese and tarragon. Mix well. Press into a 7″ (18cm) flan ring and place on a baking tray. Line with greased foil and bake for 10 minutes. Remove foil and return to oven for a further 10 minutes. Carefully transfer onto a serving plate, remove ring, and leave to cool.

3. Wash and thinly slice celery. Wipe pepper. Remove stalk and seeds. Dice into ¼″ (6mm) cubes. Wash, dry, halve, and thinly slice mushrooms.

4. Cook celery and sweetcorn, covered, in boiling salted water for 5 minutes. Add pepper and mushrooms. Simmer for a further 5 minutes. Drain, and allow to cool.

5. Melt remaining margarine. Add flour and cook for 1-2 minutes. Blend in cream, bring to the boil and simmer for 1-2 minutes. Season, cover with clingfilm and allow to cool.

6. Dice chicken into ½″ (12.5mm) cubes. Add vegetables and sauce. Mix well and pile into flan case.

Vegetable and Chicken Raised Pie

Serves 8

An impressive cold pie for picnics and packed lunches.

4 smallish carrots, approximate weight 6oz (175g)
6oz (175g) Kenya beans
4oz (125g) red pepper
8oz (225g) cooked chicken breast
1lb (450g) wholemeal flour
2 level tsps baking powder
1½ level tsps salt
¼ pint (150ml) water
4oz (125g) solid vegetable fat
1 (size 4) egg
½ pint (300ml) chicken stock
2 level tsps gelatine
1 tsp lemon juice
½ level tsp salt
pepper

1. Grease a 7½″ × 3½″ (19cm × 9cm) 2lb (900g) loaf tin. Preheat oven 220°C (425°F), gas 7.

2. Peel carrots and halve lengthways. Place in a pan of salted water, bring to the boil and simmer, covered, for 20 minutes. Drain. Top and tail beans. Wash and drain. Wipe pepper, remove stalk and seeds, quarter

lengthways. Simmer beans and pepper, covered, in salted water, for 5 minutes. Drain. Thinly slice chicken horizontally.

3. Place flour, baking powder and salt in a bowl. Mix well. Heat water and vegetable fat in a pan, bring to the boil and stir into flour. Add 2 tablespoons of warm water if necessary and mix to a stiff dough.

4. Take two thirds of the pastry, cover remainder, and keep warm. Roll out on an unfloured surface and use to line loaf tin so that pastry comes slightly above the edge. Lay red pepper over base, then half the beans, spread chicken over beans, followed by remaining beans and the carrots.

5. Lightly beat egg. Roll out remaining pastry. Brush edges with egg and place pastry lid on top. Seal and neaten edges. Garnish with pastry trimmings. Make a slit in the top, and brush with egg.

6. Bake for 25 minutes. Reduce temperature to 180°C (350°F), gas 4 and cook for a further 1 hour. Invert pie onto a baking sheet, brush edges with egg and return to oven for 15 minutes. Cool on a wire rack.

7. Dissolve gelatine in stock. Add lemon juice and seasonings. When on the point of setting, make a small hole in top of pie and drizzle in enough liquid to fill pie. Leave in refrigerator overnight to set.

Spicy Vegetable and Chicken Nuggets

Makes 20

Serve these crisp, golden nuggets with grilled tomatoes and lighty cooked runner beans.

6oz (175g) courgettes
4oz (125g) carrots
4oz (125g) cooked chicken
4oz (125g) wholemeal flour
½ level tsp salt
¼ level tsp garam masala
⅛ level tsp allspice
cayenne pepper
1 (size 3) egg
¼ pint (150ml) skimmed milk
vegetable oil for deep fat frying

1. Wipe courgettes. Grate. Peel and grate carrots. Finely chop chicken.

2. Place flour in a bowl with salt, garam masala, allspice and cayenne. Add egg and half the milk. Whisk to a smooth batter. Gradually blend in remaining milk.

3. Stir courgette, carrot and chicken into batter.

4. Heat oil for deep fat frying. Shape level tablespoonfuls of mixture into nuggets, and fry 6 at a time, for about 3-4 minutes, until crisp and golden. Drain on crumpled kitchen paper and serve at once.

Duck, Chicory and Cranberry Casserole

Serves 4

A special occasion Christmas casserole. Serve with creamed potatoes and Brussels sprouts.

5½lb (2.5kg) duck
8oz (225g) onions
8oz (225g) cranberries
1lb (450g) chicory
4 level tbsps plain flour
1 pint (600ml) chicken stock
2 level tsps soft brown sugar
1 level tsp salt
pepper
finely grated peel and juice of 1 large orange

1. Quarter duck. Trim off excess fat. Wash and pat dry. Peel and finely chop onion. Wash and drain cranberries. Wash and dry chicory, thinly slice off bases, halve lengthways.

2. Heat a large saucepan. Add duck portions and fry for 5-6 minutes on each side until crisp and brown. Remove from pan and drain off all except 3 tablespoons fat. Add onion and fry for 8-10 minutes until golden.

3. Add flour and cook for 1-2 minutes. Blend in stock, bring to the boil, stir in sugar, salt and pepper. Replace duck quarters and add cranberries, chicory and orange peel and juice. Cover, and simmer for 1-1¼ hours.

4. Preheat grill on high. Remove duck portions from pan and grill until crisp and brown, about 3-4 minutes. Serve with sauce.

Sweet and Sour Duck with Turnips

Serves 4

A tasty alternative to roasting duck is to remove its skin and simmer on the hob until tender. Jointing is then easy, and the duck is served with a tangy sweet and sour sauce, richly laden with fruit and vegetables.

5½lb (2.5kg) duck
12oz (350g) turnips
4oz (125g) onion
8oz (225g) can pineapple rings in natural juice
8oz (225g) can sliced bamboo shoots
4oz (125g) green pepper
1oz (25g) margarine
1oz (25g) cornflour
2oz (50g) soft dark brown sugar
½ level tsp ground ginger
3 tbsps malt vinegar

1 tbsp soy sauce
1 level tbsp tomato purée

1. Skin duck and remove any fat. Place in a large pan with giblets, cover with cold water, bring to the boil, cover, and simmer for 1 hour.

2. Peel turnips and dice into ¼″ (6mm) cubes. Peel and finely chop onion. Drain pineapple, reserve juice, and cut rings into 8. Drain bamboo shoots, trim to ½″ (12.5mm) strips. Wipe pepper, remove stalk and seeds, dice into ¼″ (6mm) cubes.

3. Preheat oven 180°C (350°F), gas 4. Remove duck from cooking liquor. Joint into 8 pieces. Place in a large, shallow, ovenproof dish.

4. Cook turnips in boiling water for 5 minutes. Drain. Melt margarine, add onion and cook for 2-3 minutes.

5. Mix together cornflour, sugar and ginger. Blend to a smooth paste with vinegar, soy sauce and tomato purée.

6. Make pineapple juice up to ¾ pint (450ml) with duck stock. Blend into cornflour mixture. Place in a pan with turnips, onion, pineapple, bamboo shoots and green pepper. Bring to the boil and simmer for 2-3 minutes. Pour over duck, cover with foil and bake for 35 minutes.

Turkey in Avocado and Mushroom Sauce

Serves 2

Melted Camembert or Brie provides a rich basis for this sauce. Prepare just prior to serving so that the avocado does not have to be kept hot for too long, otherwise its characteristic greenness will spoil.

2oz (50g) onion
2oz (50g) button mushrooms
4oz (125g) Camembert or Brie
2 × 5oz (150g) turkey breast fillets
2oz (50g) margarine
1 tsp vegetable oil
4oz (125g) wholemeal spaghetti
2 tbsps milk
¼ level tsp salt
pepper
1 medium avocado

1. Peel and finely chop onion. Wash, dry and quarter mushrooms. Carefully trim rind from cheese and slice cheese into four.

2. Wash and dry turkey fillets. Heat 1oz (25g) margarine and oil in a frying pan. Add turkey fillets and cook quickly on each side to seal. Reduce heat and fry gently for a further 15-20 minutes until golden and tender.

3. Bring a large pan of salted water to the boil. Add spaghetti and boil for 12-15 minutes until cooked. Drain.

4. Meanwhile, melt remaining margarine. Add onion and fry for 2-3 minutes. Add mushrooms and cook for a further 1-2 minutes. Stir in cheese, milk and seasonings. Heat gently until cheese has melted.

5. At the last minute halve avocado, remove stone and skin. Dice into ½″ (12.5mm) cubes and stir into sauce. Cook for 1-2 minutes until heated through.

6. Arrange spaghetti on a warmed serving dish. Make a border on top with the sauce. Drain turkey fillets and arrange in centre. Serve at once.

Leek, Tomato and Turkey Layer

Serves 6

Turkey often has a tendency to be slightly dry, however, by cooking it on a bed of leeks, covered with juicy tomatoes and a savoury chicken sauce, beautifully moist and succulent meat is ensured. Serve with a leafy seasonal vegetable and mashed potatoes, creamed with a little milk and nutmeg.

1lb (450g) leeks
10oz (275g) boneless and skinless turkey breast
1lb (450g) tomatoes
1oz (25g) margarine
1oz (25g) plain flour
½ pint (300ml) chicken stock
½ level tsp savory
¼ level tsp salt
4oz (125g) green streaky bacon

1. Lightly grease a 3 pint (1.8 litre) oval, shallow dish. Preheat oven 190°C (375°F), gas 5.

2. Trim leeks 1″ (2.5cm) above green stalk. Slice into ¼″ (6mm) rings. Wash and drain well. Place in base of dish.

3. Slit turkey breast almost in half, open out and place between two sheets of greaseproof paper. Hammer with a rolling pin until thin. Cut into small chunks. Place over leeks.

4. Thinly slice tomatoes and lay over turkey.

5. Melt margarine, add flour and cook for 1-2 minutes. Stir in stock. Add savory and salt. Bring to the boil and simmer for 2-3 minutes. Pour over tomatoes. Remove rind from bacon, lay strips diagonally across dish and bake, uncovered, for 1¼ hours.

INDEX